DEPRESSION AMERICA

DEPRESSION AMERICA

DEPRESSION AMERICA

Volume 2

ROOSEVELT'S FIRST TERM

GROLIER
EDUCATIONAL

About This book

The Great Depression is one of the most important periods of modern U.S. history. Images of breadlines and hungry families are as haunting today as they were at the time. Why did the crisis occur in the world's richest country, and how has it shaped the United States today? *Depression America* answers these questions and reveals a highly complex period in great detail. It describes the uplifting achievements of individuals, tells touching stories of community spirit, and illustrates a rich cultural life stretching from painting to movie-making.

Each of the six volumes covers a particular aspect of the period. The first traces the causes of the Depression through the preceding decades of U.S. history. The second examines the first term of Franklin D. Roosevelt and the New Deal he put in place to temper the effects of the crisis. The third volume studies how the Depression affected the lives of ordinary Americans. Volume 4 reveals the opposition FDR faced from both the political right and left, while Volume 5 explores the effect of the period on U.S. society and culture. The final volume places the Depression in the context of global extremism and the outbreak of World War II, the effects of which restored the United States to economic health.

Each book is split into chapters that explore their themes in depth. References within the text and in a See Also box at the end of each chapter point you to related articles elsewhere in the set, allowing you to further investigate topics of particular interest. There are also many special boxes throughout the set that highlight particular subjects in greater detail. They might provide a biography of an important person, examine the effect of a particular event, or give an eyewitness account of life in the Depression.

If you are not sure where to find a subject, look it up in the set index in each volume. The index covers all six books, so it will help you trace topics throughout the set. A glossary at the end of each book provides a brief explanation of important words and concepts, and a timeline gives a chronological account of key events of the period. The Further Reading list contains numerous books and useful web sites to allow you to do your own research.

Published 2001 by Grolier Educational
Sherman Turnpike
Danbury, Connecticut 06816

© 2001 Brown Partworks Limited

Set ISBN: 0-7172-5502-6
Volume ISBN: 0-7172-5504-2

Library of Congress Cataloging-in-Publication Data
Depression America
       p. cm.
    Includes indexes
    Contents: v. 1. Boom and bust – v. 2. Roosevelt's first term – v. 3. Countryside and city – v. 4. Political tensions – v. 5. U.S. society – v. 6. The war years and economic boom.
    ISBN 0-7172-5502-6 (set : alk. paper)
    1. United States–Economic conditions–1918-1945–Juvenile literature. 3. New Deal, 1933-1939–Juvenile literature. 4. Working class–United States–Juvenile literature. 5. United States–Social life and customs–1918-1945–Juvenile literature. [1. Depressions–1929. 2. New Deal, 1933-1939. 3. United States–History–1919-1933. 4. United States–History– 1933-1945. 5. United States–Economic conditions– 1918-1945.]

HC106.3 D44 2001
330.973'0916–dc21

                                00-046641

For information address the publisher:
Grolier Educational, Sherman Turnpike,
Danbury, Connecticut 06816

Printed and bound in Singapore

For Brown Partworks
Volume consultant:
Kenneth E. Hendrickson, Jr., Chair,
History Department, Midwestern State University
Managing editor: Tim Cooke
Editors: Claire Ellerton, Edward Horton, Christine Hatt, Lee Stacy
Designers: Sarah Williams, Lynne Ross
Picture research:
Becky Cox, Helen Simm, Daniela Marceddu
Indexer: Kay Ollerenshaw

CONTENTS

About This book   4

The Election of 1932   6

The First Hundred Days   24

The Roosevelts: A New Style   44

Where Did the Depression Bite?   64

Putting People to Work   80

The Election of 1936   98

Glossary   118

Further Reading   119

Timeline   121

Index   122

1

THE ELECTION OF 1932

As Americans went to the polls in November 1932, they knew only too well that the choice they were about to make was a fateful one. Few doubted that the result would be a crushing defeat for the Republican incumbent, Herbert Hoover, but what could the nation expect from his Democratic challenger?

The unemployment figures alone provide a graphic illustration of what was happening in the United States during the long buildup to the 1932 presidential election. At the end of 1930 the figure stood at five million. Twelve months later it was almost double that. By election day in November 1932

The famous FDR smile, on this occasion in response to reports that he was ahead in the race for the governorship of New York in 1928. He won a narrow victory.

there were more than 13 million unemployed. It was the most visible social consequence of the economic meltdown that occurred during those years. In its wake unemployment brought hunger, cold, and sickness into millions of homes. Perhaps even worse, it generated a deadening sense of despair as the months and years dragged by with no upturn in sight. Any repetition of the glib prediction that prosperity was just around the corner would have provoked hollow laughter.

At an individual level patience snapped. People looted stores for food and other necessities. At other times, and in other places, similar discontent had led to social and political breakdown. Many thoughtful observers sensed rebellion in the air. Edward O'Neal of the American Farm Bureau Federation told Congress in 1932 that "Unless something is

done for the American farmer, we will have revolution in the countryside in less than 12 months." It would have been just as plausible to utter warnings about the danger of insurrection in the coal-mining regions or the possibility of hunger riots in the streets of major cities.

Such was the background against which the election of 1932 took place. Its aftermath might determine whether the economic crisis could be solved at all by peaceful means, or whether the country would descend into anarchy and revolution.

1. ROOSEVELT'S RISE TO POWER

By 1932 Franklin Delano Roosevelt, governor of the state of New York, had risen to the top of the Democratic Party, at least in terms of his popularity with the party's grass roots and the wider

Vice-presidential candidate FDR with presidential candidate James M. Cox, campaigning in Dayton, Ohio, in 1920.

American public. His political enemies, of whom there were many, liked to portray him as a political lightweight of limited experience and modest ability, as a spoiled rich man who just thought it would be rather agreeable to be president—in short, as simply not up to the job. Some were none too delicate in drawing attention to the fact that Roosevelt was seriously disabled as the result of polio. The implication was that the White House should be occupied by an able-bodied man. With historical hindsight such a general picture appears ludicrous, but even at the time it was ridiculously wide of the mark.

Roosevelt made overtures toward running for a presidential

Al Smith's trademark derby hat makes a cute dog basket in this election photograph circulated during the 1928 campaign.

everything else for this man born with the most silvery of spoons in his mouth (see Chapter 3, "The Roosevelts: A New Style"). Not only was he rich and well born, but his name also conjured up the most popular president in living memory, his fifth cousin Theodore Roosevelt (see Volume 1, Chapter 1, "The United States, 1865–1914").

The following year, 1921, brought an abrupt halt to Roosevelt's gliding progress through life. He was stricken with polio and suffered paralysis in his legs for the rest of his life. Any political aspirations appeared to have been dashed.

FDR BEGINS HIS POLITICAL COMEBACK

Roosevelt's next appearance on the national political stage was at the 1924 Democratic party convention. He made a powerful speech nominating Governor Alfred E. Smith of New York (1873–1944) as presidential candidate. Even more memorable than the speech, however, was the image of Roosevelt, his legs locked in steel braces, slowly making his way on crutches to the podium and the beam of delight on his

election in 1920, when he was selected by the Democrats as James M. Cox's running mate. That election was a hopeless cause for the Democrats. The American public wanted a change and by 1920 had largely tired of what became one of the major issues in the campaign, U.S. membership in the newly formed League of Nations. Because the League was the inspiration of outgoing President Woodrow Wilson, the Cox-Roosevelt ticket had to back it. The result, predictably, was a Republican landslide. Nevertheless, Roosevelt gained national recognition in the course of the campaign, and at a youthful 38 his political career still stretched before him. In fact, to date his political rise had been quite effortless, seemingly like

Roosevelt's reemergence on the political stage, June 26, 1924, when he nominated Al Smith for the Democratic presidential ticket.

face as he let go of the crutches and grabbed the lectern. Smith failed to get the nomination, but Roosevelt had signaled his determination not to let his affliction force his withdrawal from public life.

The next milestone came four years later, when Smith did gain the 1928 Democratic nomination for the presidency. That left a vacancy for the governorship of New York, and Roosevelt, with some reluctance, allowed Smith to secure him the nomination. Smith went down to defeat nationally, but Roosevelt won New York by a narrow margin. Effectively, this meant that FDR was no longer in a subordinate position to his one-time political benefactor Al Smith. Henceforth a keen and, on Smith's part at least, bitter rivalry characterized the relationship between the two most popular figures in the Democratic Party.

FDR center stage and Eleanor Roosevelt (far left), with Democratic Party workers after his election as governor of New York in 1928.

THE ENERGETIC GOVERNOR

Roosevelt marked his governorship by supporting a variety of progressive legislation. He obtained tax relief for farmers, for instance and, as the Great

•

"A governor does not have to be an acrobat."

•

Depression began to bite, established the first system of relief for the unemployed in New York (see Volume 4, Chapter 5, "Welfare"). He also brought about tighter control of public utilities. New York enjoyed a huge power resource in the swirling waters of the St. Lawrence River, and Roosevelt helped create a power authority to develop hydro-electric power on the river. He also endorsed laws modernizing the prison system and helped the

elderly by establishing an old-age pension program. Conservation was another area in which FDR was active, creating, among other things, a reforestation program.

Roosevelt was an energetic and popular governor, and was reelected by a record majority in 1930. Increasingly, his physical disability appeared irrelevant to his ability to take on big challenges. As Smith had pointedly remarked when Roosevelt's health came up at a press conference during the 1928 campaign, "A governor does not have to be an acrobat." For his part Roosevelt never seemed concerned in the slightest about his disability, appearing serenely composed as he was lifted in and out of cars and trains, and the cumbersome leg braces were clamped on.

Politically, Roosevelt became increasingly liberal as the Depression took hold. In 1931 he wrote, "I believe the country is ready for a more progressive policy." In response to President Hoover's insistence that relief for the unemployed must come from

Harry Hopkins, who would go on to become a leading New Dealer, administered FDR's relief program in New York from 1931.

state and local sources rather than the federal government, Governor Roosevelt pushed through the Temporary Emergency Relief Administration. Administered by Harry Hopkins (1890–1946), who would go on to play a key role throughout FDR's White House days, TERA was the first practical government measure anywhere in the nation to alleviate the effects of unemployment.

THE BATTLE FOR THE DEMOCRATIC NOMINATION

During months of political maneuvering leading up to the 1932 Democratic National Convention, Roosevelt emerged as the front-runner, with particular strength in the South and West. In James A. Farley (1888–1976), New York Democratic Party chairman, he had an able campaign director, and Farley and Louis M. Howe (1871–1936), a long-time Roosevelt loyalist, worked ceaselessly to line up solid support for their man.

It was not an easy task. At that time the Democratic Party rules stipulated that to get the presidential nomination, a candidate had to amass the votes of two-thirds of the delegates. That was always a difficult task, and it was made more difficult on this

occasion for a peculiar reason. Having not won a presidential election for 16 years, the Democrats were desperate for victory. Under normal conditions that would have ensured that they would be eager to line up behind the candidate with the best prospects of winning. By the summer of 1932, however, it was hard to find anyone who thought the Democrats could possibly lose, no matter whom they put up. This was a measure of how low the Hoover administration had fallen in public esteem (see Volume 1, Chapter 7, "Hoover: The Search for a Solution"). So Roosevelt's well-known popularity did not guarantee him the nomination. In particular, he faced a fierce challenge from Al Smith, who could not bear to see Roosevelt snatch the prize he thought

Governor and Mrs. Roosevelt acknowledge the crowds while driving through Peekskill, N.Y., in 1929.

Assembling the Brain Trust

Raymond Moley (1886–1975), from Ohio, was the lynchpin of the Brain Trust, the group of academics largely recruited from Columbia University who helped Governor Roosevelt formulate policy in the period leading up to the elections of 1932. As a boy Moley had a precocious interest in politics, instinctively in a progressive direction. At one time he thought he would take up the socialist cause. After completing a degree in political science, however, he became an expert on criminal justice. He met Roosevelt's faithful aide Louis Howe at Columbia Law School, and Howe introduced him to the future president. Initially somewhat skeptical of the legendary charm, Moley quickly came to see that Roosevelt was completely open-minded and therefore the perfect channel for many of Moley's progressive ideas. Overall, Moley held the view that government and business should work together to devise efficient national planning policies. Only in this way could the free enterprise or capitalist system survive while curbing its worst excesses and the wastefulness of unrestrained competition.

The second of the three principal "brains" recruited to the group was Rexford Guy Tugwell (1891–1979), a dashing young economist who was an authority on agriculture. Tugwell's father grew fruit in upstate New York and owned a canning factory, so Rexford had first-hand knowledge of the economics of farming. Tugwell studied economics at the Uni-

versity of Pennsylvania. He had a fund of radical ideas, though he did not force these on Franklin Roosevelt. Moley described Tugwell as "an enormously exhilarating companion."

By May 1932 Moley had found another member of the Brain Trust. Adolf Berle, Jr. (1895–1971) came from a strongly Christian background. His father was a minister, and his maternal grandfather had done missionary work with the Sioux in South Dakota. Berle believed that progressive ideals could be incorporated in the existing economic system and was extremely eager to get into a position where he could apply such principles. In 1927 Berle took a job at Columbia Law School where he researched the way corporations affected American life; and when the call came to advise Roosevelt, he jumped at it, even though he supported a rival candidate for the Democratic nomination.

Rexford Tugwell (left), one of the most prominent members of the Brain Trust, with New Deal stalwart Harry Hopkins in 1937.

The governor of New York surrounded by advisers in 1930. His reelection that year made him a leading presidential contender.

belonged to him. There were other candidates too, but it was expected that it would finally come down to a straight fight between Roosevelt and Smith.

To bolster his candidacy, Roosevelt assembled a group of policy advisers drawn from the ranks of academics and headed up by Raymond Moley of the Columbia Law School. The advisory group was given the name Brains Trust (later shortened to Brain Trust) by a *New York Times* reporter, James Kieran.

Raymond Moley was highly influential during the campaign and helped Roosevelt draft several of his important speeches. Roosevelt had for some time been interested in the relatively new medium of radio, which most politicians tended to shy away from, and on April 7, 1932, he

delivered a 10-minute broadcast that caused a great stir. Written by Moley, the speech referred to the "forgotten man at the bottom of the economic pyramid."

Language and sentiment such as this foreshadowed the New Deal—and they reflected the way vast numbers of people were thinking. They listened with approval as Roosevelt explained that the economy had to be rebuilt from "the bottom up and not from the top down...." Roosevelt was explicitly attacking the economic theories that underpinned the Hoover administration's response to the crisis. He was saying that inaction was no longer an option, that it was unacceptable to wait for a resumption of confidence in the business community that would in turn lead to recovery further down the economic ladder—the so-called trickle-down theory. Roosevelt thought this was backward. As he saw it, those at the bottom of the pile needed purchasing power in order to stimulate demand; that

was the only way the economy could possibly revive (see Volume 4, Chapter 1, "Left vs. Right").

Many saw this as simple common sense, but for others, Democrats as well as Republicans, it had too radical a flavor. Al Smith, for example, flatly contradicted his rival: "I protest against the endeavor to delude the poor people of this country to their ruin by trying to make them believe that they can get employment before the people who would ordinarily employ them are also again restored to conditions of normal prosperity."

Some Democrats advised Roosevelt to moderate his tone, but Roosevelt gave another rousing speech only five days later at St. Paul, Minnesota. This Jefferson Day address continued in the same vein as the Forgotten Man broad-

•

"I plead not for a class control, but for a true concert of interests."

•

cast: Roosevelt advocated "a shared common life, the low as well as the high. In most of our present plans, there is too much disposition to mistake the part for the whole, the head for the body, the captain for the company, the general for the army. I plead not for a class control, but for a true concert of interests."

Roosevelt was clearly staking out a position on the left of the Democratic Party, and he was putting forward ideas that only a few years before would have found little resonance in a country that accepted free-market policies

The Bitter Loser

When Roosevelt put forward Al Smith's name at the 1924 Democratic convention, he dubbed him "the happy warrior." With his brown derby hat, ever-present cigar, and catchy theme song "The Sidewalks of New York," Smith certainly lived up to the description. But his failure to gain the nomination in 1924, heavy defeat by Hoover in 1928, and then the final humiliation of seeing Roosevelt take the prize in 1932 left him embittered. He became a carping critic of FDR's New Deal policies and in 1936 and 1940 publicly supported the Republican candidates.

of Soviet agriculture. While he rejected communist political doctrine, Tugwell came away convinced that agriculture needed long-range centralized planning if it was to avoid the cyclical boom and bust that American farmers had to endure. When in May Roosevelt made a speech at Oglethorpe University, Georgia, Tugwell's contribution was clear. Roosevelt spoke of using "drastic means" to correct the economy. He spoke out boldly against uncaring bankers and greedy businessmen.

In May 1932 Raymond Moley wrote a long memorandum in which he outlined policies that would form part of Roosevelt's New Deal. What people wanted, he explained, was "not a choice between two names for the same reactionary doctrine. The alternative should be a party of liberal thought, of planned action, and enlightened international outlook…of democratic principles."

FDR's Nomination

The Democratic National Convention opened in Chicago on June 27. Farley worked frantically behind the scenes to create the impression that Roosevelt was so far ahead in committed votes that he would clinch the nomination on the first ballot. What he was trying to do was create a bandwagon effect among the uncommitted so that his prophecy of a first-ballot win would come true. He failed. When the first ballot was held during an all-night session on July 1, the result was 666½ for Roosevelt, 203¾ for Smith, 90¼ for John Nance Garner of Texas (1868–1967), who was Speaker of the House of Representatives. The remainder of the 1,154 votes were spread among six other candidates.

It appeared that with such a handsome lead on the first ballot Roosevelt was nearly home and dry; but as Farley knew by long experience, such was not the case. Because of the two-thirds rule the

without question. Now, with the market so spectacularly having failed to sustain prosperity, there was a large and growing audience for the sort of alternative approach Roosevelt seemed to be suggesting.

However, Roosevelt seemed stronger on generalities than on specifics. For example, attractive as it was as a goal, how was purchasing power going to be given to the poor farmers? Rexford Tugwell, a leading member of the Brain Trust, stepped in. Tugwell had been a member of a trade delegation to the Soviet Union in 1927 and had been impressed with the progress

This cartoon captures Al Smith's sourness at Roosevelt's bid for the 1932 Democratic nomination, which he thought was his by right.

FDR campaigning at home, in Hyde Park, N.Y., in 1932. In fact he polled more strongly in the South and West than in his native Northeast.

Democrats had a tradition of finding their leading candidates deadlocked after a few ballots, with neither able to push past the two-thirds barrier. When that happened, sometimes after days and nights of balloting, the convention would have to consider a compromise candidate. As recently as the 1924 convention, Al Smith and William McAdoo (1863–1941), a California lawyer and railroad executive, had found themselves in such a predicament. On the 103rd ballot they had caved in and released their ballots, and the relatively unknown John W. Davis (1873–1955) was nominated. He went down to heavy defeat in the presidential elections of that year. So now Farley lobbied desperately to get those extra votes that would take his man over the top quickly, knowing that the longer the contest went on, the greater the

danger that victory would be snatched away.

On the second ballot, at 8:00 A.M., Roosevelt gained 11 votes, and on the third, held an hour later, he picked up a few more. But he still remained 89 votes short of what he needed, and it was beginning to look as if he was stalled at that level of support.

At that point the exhausted delegates adjourned until the evening. By then both Garner and McAdoo, who was not in the running himself this time and whose California delegation was committed to Garner, responded to the looming crisis. Neither man could stomach a repeat of the 1924 fiasco. So on the fourth ballot, with Garner's approval, McAdoo came to the dais to speak. He began by saying that California had come to the convention to nominate a president of the United States, not "to deadlock this convention, or to

William McAdoo delivered California's votes to Roosevelt on the fourth ballot, ensuring his nomination at the 1932 convention.

engage in another desolating contest like that of 1924...."

With that, he delivered California's votes to Roosevelt. And amid scenes of wild delight state after state joined the late bandwagon, and Roosevelt was nominated. As part of the deal that had secured him the last-minute switch, Roosevelt named Garner as his running mate. Garner, who would live on to nearly 100 years

•

"I pledge you, I pledge myself, to a new deal for the American people."

•

of age, is chiefly remembered for his graphic dismissal of the vice-presidency as "not worth a pitcher of warm spit." But "Cactus Jack" Garner spoke for all who could see the obvious when he remarked dryly that all FDR had to do to win the election was to stay alive until election day.

In a characteristically dramatic, memorable gesture, Roosevelt hired a plane and flew from Albany to accept the nomination at the convention in Chicago. The small plane battled against headwinds all the way and took nine hours to complete the journey. The waiting delegates ran out of prepared speeches and entertained themselves by singing to help pass the time until FDR arrived.

When he finally entered the hall to a standing ovation, Roosevelt was in buoyant spirits. His chosen mode of transport was, as he told the convention, "symbolic that in so doing I broke tradition. Let it be from now on the task of our party to break foolish traditions and leave it to the Republican leadership, far more skilled in that art, to break promises." The delegates relished Roosevelt's wit, and they responded too to the substance of his speech, in which he etched a memorable phrase on the consciousness of the nation: "I pledge you, I pledge myself, to a new deal for the American people."

Hoover's Reselection

The Republicans too held their nominating convention in Chicago in June 1932, a little earlier in the month. It was a lackluster affair. There was little enthusiasm for President Hoover himself and seemingly none at all for discussing how to come to grips with the crisis. It was almost as if the world outside the new Michigan Avenue stadium where the delegates were gathered did not exist. From long habit the Depression was blamed on factors external to the United States, and the Hoover administration was credited with doing a good job under difficult circumstances. The president was renominated almost by acclamation, but it is hard to see what possible alternative the convention had, since Hoover had made clear his desire to continue in office. Had they repudiated him, they would have appeared to be blaming his Republican administration for the Depression. That would have handed the election to their opponents on a plate.

On October 31 in New York City's Madison Square Garden, in one of the president's last speeches before the election, Hoover described the upcoming election as "a contest between two philosophies of government." The Democrats, Hoover claimed, "are proposing changes and so-called new deals which would destroy the very foundations of the American system of life. We denounce any attempt to stir class feeling or class antagonisms in the United States."

FDR's Brilliant Campaign

During the election campaign Roosevelt visited 38 states, as if to underline his physical fitness for the challenges ahead. Wherever he went, he radiated cheerfulness and optimism, and it proved infectious. The upbeat mood of the Roosevelt campaign was perfectly captured in its endlessly repeated theme song, "Happy Days Are Here Again."

The Depression and what the candidates proposed to do about it dominated the election cam-

Having flown to Chicago to accept the nomination, FDR, who was the first president to fly, remained an enthusiast for air travel.

Never Mind the Detail

Raymond Moley once presented Roosevelt with two quite different drafts on tariff policy. Rather than choose between them, Roosevelt calmly told Moley, to his amazement, to "weave the two together." This seeming indifference to the finer points of policy, at least prior to being in office, was remarked on by many at the time, often in tones of bewilderment or frustration.

Moley later looked back at the way ideas were flung together at the time, wryly remarking that "to look upon these policies as the result of a unified plan was to believe that the accumulation of stuffed snakes, baseball pictures, school flags, old tennis shoes, carpenter's tools, geometry books, and chemistry sets in a boy's bedroom could have been put there by an interior decorator."

FDR "pressing the flesh" in Georgia during the 1932 campaign. His easy affability in such encounters was a huge electoral asset.

paign. Even the touchy issue of Prohibition, which throughout the 1920s had split the Democrats between northern urban wets and southern rural drys, scarcely figured. The Democratic platform called for repeal, a position Roosevelt personally supported but did not think should be allowed to distract attention from the ills besetting the nation.

The main thrust of Roosevelt's campaign was to decry the inadequacy of the Hoover administration's response to the economic slump. He then contrasted that with his own upbeat analysis of what a Democratic administration would be able to achieve.

Outlining the New Deal

Some who listened to the specifics of what Roosevelt was saying thought they heard puzzling contradictions, in particular over how he intended to fund his program for national recovery. All FDR's

Under the title "An Old Idea" this 1932 cartoon credits Roosevelt with wanting to improve the plight of the hard-hit farming community.

number of specific policy commitments. He spoke of the need for public development of electric power, soil conservation, and reforestation (see Chapter 5, "Putting People to Work"). He slammed the misuse of financial power by big business and said he would curb it (see Volume 5, Chapter 1, "Government, Industry, and Economic Policy").

In a speech in Columbus, Ohio, he attacked Hoover for over-regulation and demanded more competition. Moving on to Topeka, he called for a more equitable distribution of wealth. Land use should be carefully planned. He would bring in tax reforms to aid farmers, and federal credit should be used to refinance mortgages for farmers. Wherever he went, he spoke of the responsibility the federal government must

talk about a "New Deal" made it clear that he wanted the federal government to interfere far more in the economic affairs of the nation than had previously even been contemplated in peacetime (see Chapter 2, "The First Hundred Days"). In fact Roosevelt referred repeatedly to the need for a wartime-like response to the crisis. In the Forgotten Man speech he argued that the nation was facing "a more grave emergency than in 1917." Days later in the Jefferson Day address at St. Paul he repeated that warning and then scathingly compared the Hoover administration's "panic-stricken policy of delay and improvisation with that devised to meet the emergency of war 15 years ago." He refrained from pointing out that the wartime

emergency had resulted in a huge increase in federal spending.

During the campaign FDR fleshed out his program for recovery and reform with a

FDR and his running mate John Nance Garner, seated, with the governor of Kansas and later secretary of war, Harry Woodring.

take for providing unemployment relief. Whatever their merits, policies to aid farmers and provide unemployment benefit would clearly cost money.

In Pittsburgh, however, FDR attacked the 50 percent increase in government spending since 1927, denouncing it as "the most reckless and extravagant past that I have been able to discover in the statistical record of any peacetime government anywhere, anytime." He attacked Hoover for not balancing the budget and pledged himself to a reduction in government spending of 25 percent.

Moving on to Portland, Oregon, Roosevelt made one of his more antibusiness speeches, saying that he wanted to "protect the welfare of the people against selfish greed." In Salt Lake City he sketched out a vision of federal regulation and promised aid for the railroad system. In Detroit he spoke eloquently about his wish to stamp out poverty, but refused to say how he would do it, since it was Sunday, and he said he did not want to talk politics on a Sunday!

The result of all this was to put across a message of a dynamic political agenda without providing a very clear picture of what it would be like in practice. In particular, the glaring contradiction between cutting government spending to balance the budget while spending more to relieve poverty was never satisfactorily explained. But in the course of the campaign one central message repeatedly came across loud and clear: Roosevelt and his advisers were brimful of ideas for tackling the Depression. People could take different things from his speeches, but more than anything it was the confident tone of the speeches as much as the content that caught the public imagination.

Hoover's Futile Campaign

Hoover tried in vain to pin a label of irresponsibility onto Roosevelt and his spending plans, while at the same time defending his own record. The "Great Engineer" found it unendurable that, having by his own lights done the best he could, he was portrayed as callous and uncaring. Yet when he campaigned in Detroit, he was confronted by an angry mob, and mounted police had to be called out to quell the disturbance. Hoover's tone was increasingly that of a wronged man and, as the campaign drew to a close, a tired and, finally, defeated one.

Three votes for FDR at the Hyde Park polling station on November 8, 1932, as Elliott Roosevelt joins his parents on election day.

2. FDR TRIUMPHANT

Election day was November 8, and that night Roosevelt awaited the results at New York's Biltmore Hotel. From the earliest returns it was clear that he had won a landslide victory. Such an outcome surprised nobody. In total Roosevelt received just under 23 million votes against fewer than 16 million for Hoover. He carried all but six of the 48 states, giving him a massive 472–59 margin in the electoral college. The Democrats' presidential success was mirrored at all levels. The new Senate would be composed of 59 Democrats and 37 Republicans. Gains in the House of Representatives were even more striking, leaving the final tally 312 Democrats to 123 Republicans.

It was one of the most comprehensive victories in American political history. The result represented a decisive rejection of Hoover and the party he represented, and a great personal triumph for Roosevelt. The very scale of the victory meant that the new president would come into office with unchallenged authority to implement his policies. Not only would he be bringing a great public mandate to his own position, he would furthermore have huge Democratic majorities in both houses of Congress to put through legislation.

THE INTERREGNUM CRISIS

There now followed an awkward four months during which Hoover was still in office although politically finished, while President-elect Roosevelt had all the prestige of electoral victory but not yet the levers of power in his hands. The country could only wait and see

Lame Duck Congress

The session of the 72nd Congress that convened in December 1932 was the last such "lame duck" session of an outgoing Congress. In February 1933 ratification was completed of the Twentieth Amendment to the Constitution, which said that the Congress elected in November would begin its session on the following January 3. Similarly, the presidential inauguration was brought forward from March 4 to January 20.

what the new administration would do. Meanwhile, the economy continued its downward slide, with the winter of 1932–1933 proving the gloomiest yet.

Nearly one third of the members of the so-called "lame duck" 72nd Congress had not been reelected and would therefore be leaving office along with the Hoover administration in March. This further restricted the opportunity for any constructive policy making during the so-called interregnum, the four-month period between Roosevelt's election and his inauguration.

Mutual Enmity

The situation was made even more difficult because of ill-feeling between the incoming and outgoing

The New York papers say it all, as the nation awakes on November 9, 1932, to find that it has propelled FDR into the White House.

A dinner in honor of President-elect Roosevelt given at the National Press Club in Washington, D.C., on November 22, 1932.

presidents and their entourages. Hoover considered FDR an unprincipled political chameleon and bitterly resented the way FDR had portrayed him as somehow being almost personally responsible for the Great Depression. Die-hard Republicans considered the incoming New Dealers as little better than wreckers who were determined to destroy the American way of life.

Roosevelt returned Hoover's disdain, and there was probably a personal element in this. The two men had gotten on well when they served together in the Wilson administration during World War I.

But Roosevelt's aggressive election campaign had offended the thin-skinned Hoover. He, in turn, had infuriated Roosevelt in the spring of 1932 at a White House gathering of state governors. It was a hot day, and the president kept them waiting an uncomfortably long time. Roosevelt, his legs clamped into braces, refused to take a seat and stood sweltering with his fellow governors. Whether this was deliberate cruelty by Hoover (perhaps an attempt to draw unfavorable attention to FDR's disability) is unprovable, but both FDR and Eleanor Roosevelt were convinced that it was.

Hoover Asks for Support

It was against such a background that the two men warily circled each other during the long interregnum. Shortly after the election Hoover invited Roosevelt to the White House to try and enlist his support over a foreign policy crisis. It was the old issue of war debts left over from World War I. Because Germany's economic situation was such that it was unable to meet its war reparation payments to Britain and France, they in turn were defaulting on their war loan repayments to the United States (see Volume 6, Chapter 1, "Economics and Political Extremism"). Hoover wanted Roosevelt's help in setting up a commission to look into this and related issues, but Roosevelt remained noncommittal.

On January 20, 1933, Roosevelt again was invited to the White House to discuss the country's worsening economic situation. Yet

Gunman Attempts Assassination

Giuseppe Zangara, under arrest following his attempt to assassinate Roosevelt on February 15, 1933. The mayor of Chicago was killed.

On February 15, 1933, President-elect Roosevelt spent the day on a fishing cruise aboard Vincent Astor's yacht. It was his plan then to go to Miami's Bay Front Park, where 20,000 American Legionnaires were gathered, to deliver a speech. When he arrived at the park, he stood up in his car, took a microphone in his hand, and started to chat about his fishing experience. When he had finished, he was about to pose for photographers when a man jumped onto the park bandstand and fired five shots in his direction. The Democratic mayor of Chicago, Anton Cermak, who had been standing on the running board of the car, slumped to his knees and rolled to the pavement below. He had sustained a fatal chest wound. Four other people were injured by the gunfire. A woman who was standing nearby grabbed the gunman's wrist and deflected the last shot into the air before anyone else was harmed. Then finally, a policeman knocked the gunman to the ground.

Roosevelt's would-be assassin, Giuseppe Zangara, was an Italian bricklayer from Hackensack, New Jersey. He was quoted by the policeman at the scene as saying that he would "kill every president." In Zangara's clothing was found a newspaper clipping relating the story of the assassination of President McKinley in 1901.

again he left without extending a cooperative hand to the outgoing President Hoover.

Then on February 17 Hoover wrote to Roosevelt asking him to confirm that he would make a balanced budget his top priority, even if it meant raising taxes. Such a pledge, said Hoover, would calm the panic now afflicting the banking community. In doing this even Hoover admitted that he was

asking the incoming president to scrap the New Deal before it started, but Hoover was blind to any alternative explanation of what the situation demanded. When Roosevelt refused, Hoover described him as a madman.

Finally, at the very end of this fruitless relationship Roosevelt made the traditional eve of inauguration call on his predecessor at the White House. As they had tea

together on March 3, Hoover made a final plea for joint action to stave off the banking crisis. He was wasting his breath. FDR had no intention of starting out on his journey carrying any baggage from the discredited Republican administration. He was acutely aware that his inauguration the following day was an opportunity for him to make a decisive break with the past.

FDR listens attentively to outgoing President Hoover, as they are driven from St. John's Church to the Capitol for the inauguration.

FDR Escapes Assassination

The inauguration, in fact, had very nearly been brutally called off two weeks earlier. On February 15, in Miami, an apparently mentally ill bricklayer called Giuseppe Zangara, who said he had a vision of killing a "great ruler," tried to assassinate Roosevelt (see box, page 21). Five gunshots missed their target, but several others were hit, including Mayor Anton Cermak of Chicago, who subsequently died of his wounds. Roosevelt appeared amazingly unruffled by this attack and betrayed no hint of anxiety—not even after the event when he was alone with his friends. Raymond Moley noted with incredulity that he could find "not so much as the twitching of a muscle, the mopping of a brow, even the hint of a false gaiety" in the president-elect.

THE INAUGURAL ADDRESS

Saturday, March 4, 1933, was a cloudy day. President Hoover and the president-elect drove together to the Capitol. Roosevelt made his slow, awkward progress out onto the white inaugural stand to take the oath of office, repeating the words after Chief Justice Hughes. Then he turned to face the throng below. There was absolute quiet as the president began to speak.

He began by saying that he intended to be absolutely candid about the current situation. He

•

"…the only thing we have to fear is fear itself."

•

followed this with a confident assertion: "This great nation will endure as it has endured, will revive, and will prosper." Then, in ringing

tones that reached out to millions of Americans glued to radios across the land, Roosevelt launched into his theme. "So, first of all, let me assert my firm belief that

•

"This nation asks for action, and action now."

•

the only thing we have to fear is fear itself—nameless, unreasoning, unjustified terror which paralyzes needed efforts to convert retreat into advance." He then lashed into those he held responsible for the situation. "Plenty is at our doorstep, but a generous use of it languishes in the very sight of the supply. Primarily this is because rulers of the exchange of mankind's goods have failed through their own stubbornness and their own incompetence, have admitted their failure, and have abdicated.... The money changers have fled from their high seats in the temples of our civilization. We may now restore that temple to the ancient truths." Replacing greed with nobler social aspirations would not be enough, however. "This nation asks for action, and action now." This was delivered with the fervor of a call to arms.

"Our greatest primary task is to put people to work." This would be partly accomplished by "direct recruiting by the government itself." Resources would have to be better used, purchasing power raised, the expenses of government pared down. There would have to be measures to prevent foreclosures on farms and houses, and for the unemployed and destitute there would have to be coordinated efforts for relief. There must be "an end to speculation with other people's money."

The crisis at home had to be resolved before grappling with the international aspects of the crisis, which, he said, though of course they were important, "are in point of time and necessity secondary to the establishment of a sound national economy."

Finally he committed himself to national recovery above any other consideration—including the balance of power between the executive and Congress. If necessary, he would seek "broad executive power to wage a war against the emergency, as great as the power that would be given to me if we were in fact invaded by a foreign foe."

Eleanor Roosevelt afterward told reporters, "It was very, very solemn, and a little terrifying. The crowds were so tremendous, and you felt that they would do anything—if only someone would tell them what to do." Having concluded, Roosevelt waved to the cheering crowd, and suddenly his face lit up with an incandescent smile.

SEE ALSO

◆ Volume 1, Chapter 7, Hoover: The Search for a Solution

◆ Volume 2, Chapter 2, The First Hundred Days

◆ Volume 2, Chapter 3, The Roosevelts: A New Style

◆ Volume 2, Chapter 5, Putting People to Work

◆ Volume 4, Chapter 1, Left vs. Right

◆ Volume 5, Chapter 1, Government, Industry, and Economic Policy

THE FIRST HUNDRED DAYS

Immediately upon taking office, President Roosevelt summoned Congress into special session to enact emergency legislation. The result, in a hundred days of furious activity, was to lay the foundations of the New Deal.

Americans had little time to digest Franklin Roosevelt's inaugural address on March 4, 1933, before its meaning became clear enough. In particular, they realized that when the new president said, "This nation asks for action, and action now," he meant it. Even as he spoke, it was widely noted that the spirits of those millions listening to him on the radio seemed to lift. That lift, however, real though it was and desperately needed, would not be sustained through rhetoric alone.

By March 1933 spirits were low for good reason. By any

March 4, 1933: The Roosevelts leave the inauguration ceremony accompanied by Senate Majority Leader Joseph Robinson.

measure the objective situation was dire. Some 25 percent of the national work force was out of work. Unemployment left

A banquet at the governor's mansion in Albany, New York, with FDR's successor, Herbert Lehman, seated on the extreme right.

an uneven trail of despair, both geographically and in industry terms (see Chapter 4, "Where Did the Depression Bite?"). In Detroit the figure was 50 percent—a reflection of the calamity that had overwhelmed the

•

"This nation asks for action, and action now."

•

automobile industry. Car production was down 65 percent from 1929 levels. The construction industry seemed to be headed for extinction, with 75 percent of its work force unemployed.

Farmers, by the nature of their work, are rarely unemployed, so they did not swell the soaring jobless totals. But if anything their plight was even worse than that of the industrial unemployed (see Volume 3, Chapter 2, "Shadow over the Countryside"). The prosperity of the 1920s had passed the farmers by, with incomes consistently below pre-World War I levels. The Great Depression dropped the rural income by a further 60 percent. With prices for their produce at rock bottom, farmers faced foreclosure on their mortgages and destitution. There were sporadic violent clashes as bailiffs met with resistance during evictions.

1. THE CRISIS FACING PRESIDENT ROOSEVELT

However grim though this backdrop was on Inauguration Day, there was an immediate crisis that threatened to bring the nation to its knees. The American banking system was in free fall. If it should collapse, and many thought it would, the repercussions would be appalling. Savings would be wiped out and commerce crippled.

The bank crisis had been long in coming. Throughout the booming 1920s there had been a rash of bank failures—about 6,000 in the course of the decade. This was clear indication that there was something wrong with the U.S. banking system, but in the heady days of prosperity the warning went unnoticed (see Volume 1, Chapter 5, "The Fantasy World").

When the Great Depression began to bite, the rate of bank failures rose, and the Hoover administration's attempts to stem the tide were ineffectual. The fundamental problem was that there was no single authority responsible for supervising the banks. The responsibility was shared between the federal and state governments. In practice, this dual authority meant almost no authority at all. In the aftermath of the Stock Market Crash of 1929 it emerged that the banks had irresponsibly speculated with savers' money, and a number of highly placed bankers were found to have acted illegally.

Between Roosevelt's election in November 1932 and his

The First Hundred Days

The term the press used to describe the period of immense legislative activity from March 9 to June 16 1933 was lifted from history. On March 1, 1815, Napoleon Bonaparte returned from exile on the island of Elba and regained power in France. The period of upheaval that followed, which ended in his defeat at the Battle of Waterloo on June 15, is called "the hundred days."

inauguration the following March the situation steadily deteriorated. As banks failed in record numbers, public confidence in the banking system eroded. In panic, people withdrew their savings and hoarded both currency and gold. In mid-February 1933 the state of Michigan closed its banks to prevent a run on funds. In the days leading up to the inauguration state after state followed Michigan's example. During the final week of the Hoover administration $1.5 billion was withdrawn from banks in those states that still had them open for business.

THE NATION WAITS

As the crisis lurched on, Hoover tried to enlist Roosevelt's support for emergency measures to stabilize the banks. In particular Hoover wanted to declare a national bank holiday, to give the banking system breathing space. Roosevelt refused to cooperate, since he did not want to begin his administration carrying any responsibility for the mess he was inheriting. Late in the evening of March 3, however, the combined forces of the outgoing and incoming adminis-

trations tried to stave off collapse. They contacted the governors of those states that still had functioning banks and asked them to close

•

"No cosmic dramatist could possibly devise a better entrance…"

•

them in the morning. As New York and Illinois fell into line (the latter at 3:30 A.M.), Inauguration Day dawned with not a single bank open in the United States. As if to dim the lights before the curtain went up, the New York Stock Exchange too closed its doors.

A cartoon from January 30, 1933, pokes fun at the confusion spread by conflicting theories for curing the Depression.

Frantic depositors outside the closed doors of the Central National Bank in St. Petersburg, Florida, in June 1930. The bank had failed.

Robert Sherwood, a celebrated playwright and later speechwriter for FDR, put the events of that day in a vivid theatrical context. "No cosmic dramatist," Sherwood wrote, "could possibly devise a better entrance for a new President—or a new Dictator, or a new Messiah—than that accorded to Franklin Delano Roosevelt."

Congress Summoned

Having flayed the bankers in the course of his inaugural speech, Roosevelt moved swiftly to save them from the disaster he believed they had largely brought on themselves. The day following the inauguration he issued a proclamation summoning the Congress into an extraordinary session on March 9. Next day, the sixth, he proclaimed a national bank holiday from that day until the ninth. This was in effect no more than to formalize the situation as

Roosevelt's First Cabinet

Roosevelt had chosen the members of his cabinet in advance of his inauguration. They would play key roles in launching and steering the New Deal.

Henry A. Wallace (1888–1965) of Iowa was secretary of agriculture. A leading figure in farming circles, Wallace went on to serve as vice-president (1941–1945) and secretary of commerce (1945). In 1948 he ran for president as the candidate of the Progressive Party.

Harold Ickes (1874–1953) of Chicago was secretary of the interior. A gifted administrator though prickly personality, he served in his post throughout the Roosevelt years and for a year following FDR's death in 1945.

Virginian Claude Swanson (1862–1939) was secretary of the Navy. He had been chairman of the Senate Committee on Naval Affairs during World War I.

Jim Farley (1888–1976) of New York was postmaster general. He had managed FDR's successful gubernatorial campaigns in 1928 and 1930 and his 1932 presidential campaign. He would repeat that in 1936, making him the most successful campaign manager ever.

Standing (from left): Wallace, Ickes, Swanson, Farley, Roper, Perkins. Seated (from left): Dern, Hull, FDR, Woodin, Cummings.

Dan Roper (1867–1943) of South Carolina was secretary of commerce. He oversaw the administration of the NRA.

Frances Perkins (1882–1965) of Massachusetts was secretary of labor. The first woman cabinet member, she was highly effective and served throughout FDR's presidency.

George Dern (1872–1936) of Utah was secretary of war. In that capacity he supervised the participation of the Army in the CCC.

Cordell Hull (1871–1955) of Tennessee was secretary of state. He served for a record 11 years and won the Nobel Peace Prize in 1945.

William Woodin (1868–1934) of Pennsylvania was secretary of the treasury. He had given $10,000 to FDR's campaign and had a key role in resolving the banking crisis of 1933.

Homer Cummings (1870–1956) of Connecticut was attorney general. His six years in office saw many clashes between the Roosevelt administration and the Supreme Court.

Wall Street, March 13, 1933, as the banks reopened. Deposits exceeded withdrawals that day, ending the immediate banking crisis.

it existed on the fourth, and indeed in compliance with Hoover's plan, but Roosevelt's decree had a noticeably calming effect.

People coped with cash shortages as best they could. Those living in states near the Canadian border used Canadian dollars. In the Southwest they used Mexican pesos; some organizations issued credit notes, and the Dow Chemical Company paid its workers in coins they made from a magnesium alloy called Dowmetal.

Emergency Package

Meanwhile, the Treasury Department worked day and night to hammer out a rescue package for the banks that would restore confidence and enable them to reopen. The deadline was noon on the ninth, when the new Congress was scheduled to convene. With

hours to spare, the Emergency Banking Relief Act was ready and immediately put before Congress. There had been no time to print it, so it was simply read out first in the House, where it was approved in the afternoon, and then in the Senate, where it passed by a vote of 73 to 7 just after 7:00 P.M. At 8:36 that same evening Roosevelt signed it into law. The Hundred Days were off to a flying start.

The new legislation authorized the actions the president had taken over the previous few days. By proclamation the bank holiday was extended to March 13, during which time the secretary of the treasury would determine which banks were sound enough to reopen and which should remain closed. Banks that were fundamentally sound would receive funds from the Reconstruction Finance Corporation to tide them over their cash crisis, and the Federal Reserve Board was authorized to print money to ease the acute currency shortage.

Addressing the Nation

On the evening of March 12, a Sunday, President Roosevelt delivered the first of his "fireside chats," a 20-minute radio broadcast carried by all major networks into millions of homes across the nation. He began by saying simply and in a conversational tone, "I want to talk for a few minutes with the people of the United States about banking...." And so he did, explaining in everyday language how the emergency bill would operate and why he believed it would resolve the banking crisis.

On Monday morning banks began reopening, and there was no stampede to withdraw money.

Out of Cash

Roosevelt's son Elliott tells an anecdote that reveals how critical the cash situation was during the bank holiday. With no banks open, how could anyone withdraw money? Elliott set off from New York with his wife to drive to Arizona. They had only $32 dollars between them—nowhere near enough for such a journey. Elliott called his father from Little Rock, Arkansas, to ask his advice, but the president told him that he was in no position to help—he himself had only $8! As it happened, Elliott Roosevelt was diverted to Dallas, Texas, where he was welcomed by a group of businessmen who were eager to make an impression on the president's son. The penniless couple were looked after in royal style.

Female Power in the White House

One intriguing feature of the Roosevelt presidency, apparent right from the start, was the influence of women in his White House. To begin with there was no precedent for a First Lady with such a powerful political voice as Eleanor Roosevelt (1882–1962). She was a committed reforming Democrat and had been one of FDR's most influential advisers during his rise to prominence and power. So when she entered the White House, there was no question of Eleanor Roosevelt following the traditional role of domestic management and political silence. Only two days after the inauguration she gave a press conference, the first First Lady to do so.

In the course of her long tenure at the White House Eleanor Roosevelt held a huge total of 348 press conferences. She campaigned tirelessly for the rights of women and blacks, and traveled the country continually, investigating living and working conditions and reporting back to her husband. She was a hardworking journalist and promoted her views in many magazine articles. In the public mind Eleanor Roosevelt was as closely identified with the New Deal as any of the New Deal cabinet, and even the president himself.

The second powerful woman in FDR's councils was Frances Perkins, the secretary of labor and the first woman ever appointed to the cabinet. She had a background in social work, rather than experience with labor unions, the normal background for that sensitive position. She was an authority on urban living conditions and became a forceful advocate of protective legislation for the poor. The fact that she remained in her post for the entire Roosevelt presidency was an indication of how much FDR valued her contribution.

The third influential female in the Roosevelt entourage was Marguerite "Missy" LeHand (1898–1944). She had already been FDR's secretary for 13 years before he became president. Fiercely loyal and protective, she managed Roosevelt's schedule and supervised the office staff. She served as White House hostess during Eleanor Roosevelt's frequent absences, and her extremely close relationship with the president provoked considerable gossip. In time the long-lasting friendship between the First Lady and Missy LeHand cooled. But whatever the personal strains that may have been caused by LeHand's influence in the White House, the two women retained a productive working relationship.

Mrs. Roosevelt speaking at a camp for unemployed women at Bear Mountain, N.Y., in August 1933.

On the contrary, by the close of business that day deposits exceeded withdrawals. Within a few weeks more than $1 billion of hoarded money had been redeposited in banks. By the end of June around 90 percent of the nation's banks were open again.

Trimming Government Costs

On the second of the Hundred Days, March 10, Roosevelt sent a message to Congress saying in effect that the federal government was in danger of going broke, and setting out his plans to cut government spending by $4 billion. This was in line with his election promise to cut government spending (see Chapter 1, "The Election of 1932"), but saving on such a scale meant real cutbacks where they hurt—for example, government salaries. Most vocally, the American Legion and other veterans' organizations raised a huge outcry about FDR's determination to slash $400 million from veterans' pensions.

The economy bill delighted conservative commentators because it showed that the president shared their thinking about the need for a tight fiscal policy. It indicated that he was serious about trying to achieve a balanced budget. But it dismayed many Democrats, and the economy bill looked like it might get stalled in the Senate. So on March 13 Roosevelt, having remarked that "I think this would be a good time for beer," caught Congress off guard by sending down a proposal to legalize beer and light wines.

This was an immensely popular measure. Congress had already, before FDR's accession, voted to repeal the Eighteenth Amendment (Prohibition), and it was just a matter of time before the states ratified. Apart from the minority of teetotallers, Americans considered the immediate legalization of beer something to celebrate—with beer, of course. Roosevelt cunningly arranged procedures so that the economy bill would have to be passed before the beer bill was enacted. The Senate resistance to the former collapsed. The economy bill was passed on the fifteenth, the beer bill the following day.

The Hundred Days: A Summary

From March 9, 1933, when it came into session to June 16—the Hundred Days—Congress passed 15 major pieces of legislation and laid the foundations of Roosevelt's New Deal:

March 9	Emergency Banking Relief Act
March 20	Economy Act
March 22	Beer-Wine Revenue Act
March 31	Civilian Conservation Corps Reforestation Relief Act
May 12	Federal Emergency Relief Act (FERA)
May 12	Agricultural Adjustment Administration (AAA)
May 18	Tennessee Valley Authority (TVA)
May 25	Federal Securities Act
June 5	Gold Repeal Joint Resolution
June 6	National Employment System Act
June 13	Home Owners Refinancing Act
June 16	Banking Act
June 16	Farm Credit Act
June 16	Emergency Railroad Transportation Act
June 16	National Industrial Recovery Act (NIRA)

The Savior of Capitalism

The successful resolution of the banking crisis was a pivotal moment in American history. Roosevelt's long-time campaign manager Jim Farley later said that in the eight days following his inauguration the president saved capitalism. Certainly, some critics on the left were convinced and disappointed that FDR had let a golden opportunity pass to nationalize the banks. Had that been his intention, there is little doubt that he would have been able to carry even so radical a measure through Congress. An indication of the mood on Capitol Hill on March 9 is provided by the tone of the debate in the House. It lasted only 40 minutes, and during that briefest of debates there were repeated shouts of "Vote! Vote!" The Republican leader on the floor, Bertrand H. Snell, was passionate in his support for the bill, claiming that "The house is burning down and the president of the United States says this is the way to put out the fire."

Beer went on legal sale for the first time in 13 years on April 7. In St. Louis sirens and whistles sounded; in Milwaukee drinkers stood on the roofs of cars singing "Sweet Adeline."

Roosevelt had intended to adjourn the special session of Congress as soon as the emergency banking and economy bills were passed (the beer bill was just a clever tactical move). Adjournment would give his new team time to prepare a full legislative program, whereupon he would recall Congress. However, on March 16 the president had a change of mind. He had a Congress that could hardly wait to approve his plans for national

recovery. He had a press that was virtually unanimous in singing his praises. Telegrams of support were pouring into the White House at the rate of 10,000 a week. As one aide put it, "The outside public seems to behave as if Angel Gabriel had come to earth." Roosevelt decided to strike while the iron was so scorchingly hot.

•

"I think this would be a good time for beer"

•

Do Something!

As FDR swung into action, the president of Thomas A. Edison, Inc., of New Jersey, pinned up this notice:

"President Roosevelt has done his part: now you do something!

"Buy something—buy anything, anywhere; paint your kitchen, send a telegram, give a party, get a car, pay a bill, rent a flat, fix your roof, get a haircut, see a show, build a house, take a trip, sing a song, get married.

"It does not matter what you do—but get going and keep going. This old world is starting to move."

2. ROLLING OUT THE NEW DEAL

On the sixteenth FDR signaled his intention to plow ahead by sending Congress proposals for the relief of agriculture. This was a top priority for Roosevelt, and the omnibus Farm Relief Act that he finally signed into law on May 12 was the most far-reaching the nation had ever seen. It was one of the key provisions of the New Deal.

A familiar pattern began to emerge during the Hundred Days. Every few days a new measure would come down to Congress from the White House, having been hastily thrown together by the relevant department, or the Brain Trust, or the army of eager and on the whole young advisers

A beaming bartender serves the first legal beers for 13 years. FDR's decision to legalize the beverage at once created a mood of euphoria.

and officials competing for the president's attention. No one in the House or Senate knew what was coming until it arrived, nor did anyone know when the torrent of new proposals would end. Congress would immediately debate the proposal, for a longer or shorter time depending on how much opposition it stirred up. But it did so under great pressure since the next presidential proposal could arrive at any moment. Furthermore, although the 73rd Congress was by no means willing simply to "rubber stamp" every proposal sent to it by the president, its own mood, and more importantly the mood of the nation, made any serious obstruc-tion of the program unthinkable. So the Hundred Days rolled on, and so the New Deal took shape.

RELIEF FOR FARMERS

The Farm Relief Act provides a good example of the various elements that made up the New Deal. One of the most commonly used phrases at the time to describe aims of the New Deal was "relief, recovery, and reform." Relief meant just that: measures to save individuals and businesses from imminent disaster—bank-ruptcy, homelessness, hunger, even starvation. All relief measures had a sense of great urgency about them because they were aimed at warding off immediate perils. To use an analogy, relief was the despatch of fire engines in response to a 911 call. Recovery was just as vital, but more of a medium-term goal. It meant getting the American economy back on its feet, getting the wheels of industry turning again, thereby restoring prosperity for both individuals and the business community at large. To continue the analogy, it meant repairing the fire damage. The third of the three Rs, reform, was a longer-term goal. It meant

A farming family in Ozark County, Arkansas, in February 1933. Rural hardship during the darkest days of the Depression provoked despair.

Secretary of Commerce Daniel Roper (left) and Secretary of Agriculture Henry Wallace (right) at a White House conference.

Desperation

The Emergency Farm Mortgage Act was a response to acute human distress. In just one of many volatile incidents, in April 1933 Judge Charles C. Bradley was sitting in his courtroom in LeMars, Iowa. He was about to sign mortgage foreclosure notices on some local farmers' properties. In desperation the farmers stormed into the courtroom and nearly lynched him. Farmers called a national strike for May 13. However, one day before that, Congress passed the Farm Relief bill, and the strike did not materialize.

making changes in the way the American economic system operated to ensure that such a calamity as the Great Depression could never happen again. The fundamental assumption behind reform was that the Depression could have been prevented, just as fires can be prevented if appropriate safeguards are put in place and enforced.

In reality, the complexity of the nation's economy was such that the three Rs were never as neatly separated as that. So that while some New Deal measures were quite clearly relief measures, others recovery, and others specifically reform measures, most of them had a mixture of these

elements. That was certainly the case with the Farm Relief Act.

The act combined two bills. One was the Emergency Farm Mortgage Act, which enabled banks to restructure existing farm mortgages on easier terms for the farmers, with the government underwriting the cost. The second created the Agricultural Adjustment Administration. The AAA was set up to oversee an ambitious plan to raise farm incomes by restricting production.

Overproduction was at the root of the American agriculture problem. Huge surpluses had depressed prices throughout the 1920s, and the situation had become much worse during the Depression as urban poverty lessened domestic demand, and the global slump drastically curtailed exports. The idea was to restrict production by persuading farmers to take some of their acreage out of production. It applied to seven basic commodities: wheat, cotton, corn, hogs, rice, tobacco, and milk.

In return for their cooperation farmers would be paid subsidies, funded from new taxes on the processing of those farm products (such as milling flour or canning meat). The goal was to restore the purchasing power of farmers to pre-World War I levels. Chester Davis, head of the AAA in 1934, spelled out the purpose of the policy: "It is intended that the effects of improved prices of the basic crops will be reflected in better prices for other farm products and in increased employment in the cities as the farmers regain the ability to buy goods of mills and factories."

Crop restriction and subsidy ran directly counter to the American tradition of free market economics (see Volume 4, Chapter 1, "Left vs. Right"), and it was the subject of much controversy, not least among farmers themselves. Nevertheless, national

Members of the Reconstruction Finance Corporation discuss fiscal policy at a hearing of the Senate banking and currency committee.

planning of agriculture through restriction and subsidy became a permanent feature of U.S. life.

MONETARY POLICY

The debate about how best to alleviate the crisis in agriculture involved an even larger issue that lay at the heart of the American and indeed the world economic system. This was monetary policy, meaning the regulation of the money supply. Monetary policy was traditionally the province of the Federal Reserve Board, but Roosevelt was determined to wrest power from the Federal Reserve and exercise it himself, through Congress.

"Dr. Roosevelt" administers a dose of medicine to the dollar in this cartoon published in October 1939.

Even before his inauguration, Roosevelt was coming around to the idea that the money supply needed to be expanded. In other words, the total amount of money in circulation and on deposit in banks should be increased. The effect of an expansionary monetary policy would be inflation; but since the Depression had been accompanied by savage deflation, perhaps a little controlled inflation would stimulate economic recovery. According to theory, inflation would raise prices and stimulate demand for goods and services.

There was widespread support from many sectors—banking as well as manufacturing—for an expansionary monetary policy. The Reconstruction Finance Corporation (RFC) had been set up in the dying days of the Hoover administration to provide loans to banks. Roosevelt, as part of the Emergency Banking Act, enabled the RFC to go further and invest directly in banks in an attempt to get them to increase their lending—in other words, to loosen up their monetary policy. Nowhere were there voices crying out more loudly for this than in the agricultural community. Farmers were desperate to break out of the stranglehold of depressed agricultural prices. Inflation would both boost their incomes and ease their debt repayment.

Increasing the Money Supply

In fact, the president's very first action in office had been expansionary. By restoring confidence in the national banking system, he encouraged people to entrust their funds to the banks rather than hoard them. Increased funds in turn enabled the banks to increase their lending, which effectively increased the money supply.

•

"…increased employment in the cities…"

•

The entire thrust of the Hundred Days legislation was expansionary, involving as it did measures aimed at reestablishing solvency, boosting business confidence, and involving direct federal spending toward both relief and recovery. Most economists credit the expansionary monetary policy with a major role in the steady improvement in the nation's economic performance throughout the New Deal years.

The International Dimension

U.S. monetary policy had an impact far beyond America's shores. FDR took office at a time of great turmoil in the international economic system. Until very recently the world's currencies had been locked into the gold standard, which meant that their value relative to one another was

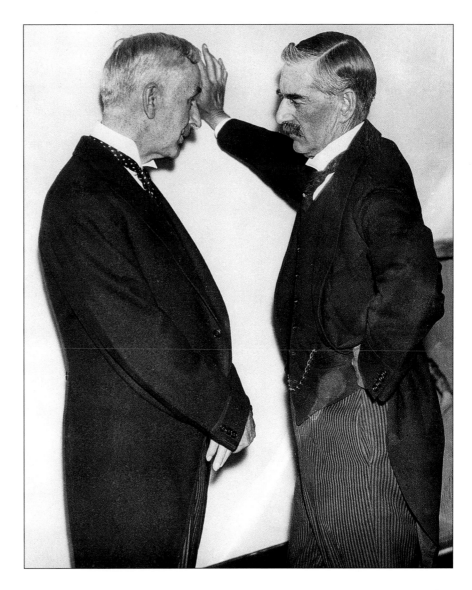

Secretary of State Cordell Hull (left) with British chancellor of the exchequer Neville Chamberlain at the 1933 London Economic Conference.

set by their value in terms of gold, into which they could be converted. This made for stable exchange rates, which in turn facilitated international trade.

By 1933 this long-standing world economic order was in disarray. Great Britain, hard hit by the Depression, had abandoned the gold standard in 1931 in order to devalue its currency and so boost exports. More and more countries were following Britain's example as they struggled

desperately for a share of shrinking world trade. Indeed, on April 18, 1933, Roosevelt had curtailed the right to convert dollars into gold—thereby effectively taking the U.S. off the gold standard. Without the universal gold standard exchange rates became unstable, and international trade suffered further.

Failure in London

In June 1933 a major international conference took place in London to try and find a way out of the dilemma. The U.S. delegation to the London Economic Conference, on FDR's instructions, refused to accept French demands

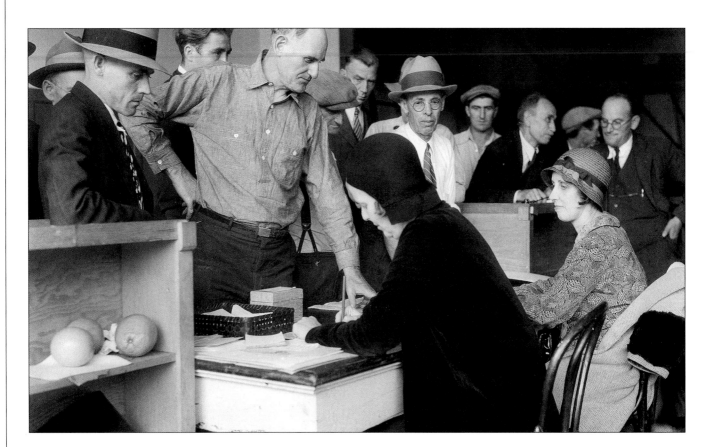

that the gold standard be re-established as a means of stabilizing currencies.

It was Roosevelt's contention that each nation should concern itself with putting its own economic house in order, as he intended to do in the U.S. with his expansionary policies. National needs, in other words, had to take precedence over international cooperation. Without American support for an agreed policy the London Economic Conference ended in failure, and the global crisis remained unresolved.

UNEMPLOYMENT RELIEF

Roosevelt had made it plain in the course of the election campaign that he considered unemployment relief to be the concern of the federal government. This had been a point of sharp contrast with President Hoover, who remained firm in his view that unemployment relief was a matter

for state and local agencies. By the spring of 1933 the scale of unemployment was so great that it constituted an emergency, and its relief by federal action was widely anticipated and approved. Indeed, the Roosevelt landslide made it a political imperative (see Chapter 5, "Putting People to Work").

On May 12, 1933, Congress approved the Federal Emergency Relief Act, which created the Federal Emergency Relief Administration (FERA). Ten days later FERA became operational under the direction of Harry L. Hopkins (1890–1946), who had served Roosevelt in a similar capacity when he was governor of New York. Hopkins was a man of remarkable dynamism. He held many important posts throughout the Roosevelt presidency, and in all of them he was conspicuous for his energy, his hatred of red tape, and his sheer enthusiasm for getting things done. Years later, during

Unemployed register for jobs in Los Angeles in September 1932. One of FDR's priorities was to put federal funds into unemployment relief.

Natural Attractions

Among its many tasks the Tennessee Valley Authority was charged with improving forestry practices in the region (FDR was keenly interested in this matter), and millions of pine saplings were planted. As well, the creation of many lovely lakes as a result of controlling the water flow led to a great increase in outdoor recreational activities. Boating, fishing, and camping would create a major leisure industry.

World War II, when he had many dealings with Hopkins, British prime minister Winston Churchill affectionately dubbed him "Lord Root of the Matter." Hopkins went to work with a will. On his first day in office he distributed millions of dollars to the individual states to shore up their attempts at providing unemployment relief. This was the beginning of the biggest relief program in American history. The FERA was funded to the tune of $500 million by Congress.

HELPING HOMEOWNERS

Like farm foreclosures, house repossession was at crisis point. In 1932 alone 250,000 homes were lost because the owners could not keep up the mortgage payments. In early 1933 this distressing occurrence was taking place more than 1,000 times a day.

The Home Owners Loan Act passed into law near the end of the Hundred Days, on June 13, 1933. It established the Home Owners Loan Corporation (HOLC), which underpinned the housing mortgage market in the same way as the Emergency Farm Mortgage Act underpinned farm mortgages. The morning the Home Owners' Loan Corporation opened its doors, 500 people crowded in to refinance their mortgages. During its first three years of operation HOLC spent in excess of $3 billion to refinance more than a million homes.

THE TENNESSEE VALLEY AUTHORITY

Perhaps the most radical of all the measures that the president and Congress implemented during the Hundred Days was the establishment of the Tennessee Valley Authority (TVA) (see box, page 92). In fact, the controversies that embroiled the project exposed a number of the fault lines in modern American history.

The Tennessee River is the fifth largest in the United States in terms of volume of stream flow. It rises in the southern Appalachians and runs for about 650 miles, joining the Ohio River at Paducah, Kentucky. Its drainage basin includes parts of seven states, and the Tennessee River runs through some of the historically most economically disadvantaged, though physically beautiful, areas of the country.

Construction workers at the Norris Dam site in Tennessee in 1933, where they are building a bridge over the Clinch River, a TVA project.

The TVA Norris Dam hydroelectric installation on the Clinch River, a tributary of the Tennessee, which was completed in 1936.

Midway on its journey, at Muscle Shoals, Alabama, rapids made the Tennessee unnavigable. From the late 19th century there were a number of attempts, both private and at state level, to deal with the shoals. None succeeded. Then during World War I President Woodrow Wilson backed a plan to build nitrate manufacturing plants at Muscle Shoals, which involved constructing dams to harness hydroelectric power. Nitrates were essential for making munitions, and Wilson believed the United States should have its own domestic supply rather than having to rely on imports from Chile.

The war ended with the Muscle Shoals scheme far from finished, and throughout the 1920s there was much wrangling about who should do what about the situation. There were attempts to end the government's involvement and investment in Muscle Shoals, but Congress blocked them. From the completely opposite position came no fewer than six bills proposed by Senator George W. Norris of Nebraska. Although a Republican, Norris was fiercely opposed to the sale of the government's Muscle Shoals assets to the private sector.

•

"He is more than with me... he has plans to go even farther than I did!"

•

As he saw it, whoever got hold of the project would have a particular agenda. There were some who wanted to manufacture fertilizer from nitrates; others were concerned solely with hydroelectric power; still others were preoccupied by soil erosion; and some were interested only in flood control. Norris took the view that no single interest, however worthy, should dictate the development of the Muscle Shoals resource. He wanted the federal government to

Plenty—or the Simple Life?

The contradictory nature of Americans' perceptions of business and industry was expressed by the journalist Dorothy Thompson, writing in 1938: "Two souls dwell within the bosom of the American people. The one loves the Abundant Life, as expressed in the cheap and plentiful products of large-scale mass production and distribution.... The other soul yearns for former simplicities, for decentralization, for the interests of the 'little man,' revolts against high-pressure salesmanship, denounces 'monopoly' and 'economic empires,' and seeks means of breaking them up." How was one industrial recovery bill to encompass both attitudes?

accept overall responsibility for the Muscle Shoals development so that its use could be rationally planned for many purposes. Each of Norris's bills was vetoed by the

•

"...planning for

the generations

to come"

•

Republican presidents Coolidge and Hoover.

In the Democrat Roosevelt, however, Norris now found an ally. Before he took office, the

The mighty Wilson Dam at Muscle Shoals, Alabama, was built before the formation of the TVA, but was incorporated into the program.

president-elect toured the Tennessee Valley with the senator. When reporters afterward interviewed Norris, they asked him, "Is he really with you?" A stunned Norris replied, "He is more than with me, because he plans to go even farther than I did!"

The Tennessee Valley was a chronically poor area and had been devastated by the effects of the Great Depression. Its towns and cities were at constant risk from flooding, and malaria was rife. Malnutrition was a simple fact of

life. For Roosevelt here was a golden opportunity to tackle several problems at once. The Muscle Shoals project provided "an opportunity of setting an example of planning, planning not just for ourselves but planning for the generations to come, tying in industry and agriculture and forestry and flood prevention." Norris prepared a bill in Congress, and Roosevelt duly signed the TVA into existence on May 18, 1933.

The TVA would build dams, providing water for irrigation, controlling floods, and generating cheap hydroelectric power. The price of the cheap power would set a benchmark for private power companies. There would be soil reclamation in the valley, making

it possible to grow crops and trees on land that had previously been too poor. There would be social and educational programs to improve the lives of the residents. The project affected an area of 40,000 square miles.

The TVA was a federal agency, but built into it was a great deal of flexibility that gave local inhabitants a say in the running of the project. This made it very popular at ground level, although inevitably there were critics of its creation. It clearly signaled the government's intention to take a direct role in a major industry—power generation—in the public interest. This was bound to antagonize conservatives, who said that the project smacked of socialism and worse.

Representative Joe Martin of Massachusetts, an implacable foe

The NRA Blue Eagle cropped up everywhere—including here on a Miami beach in September 1933 in a promotional stunt.

of the New Deal, said the TVA was "patterned closely after one of the Soviet dreams." Roosevelt shrugged off such charges. When asked to explain the philosophy behind the project, Roosevelt described it as "neither fish nor fowl, but whatever it is, it will taste awfully good to the people of the Tennessee Valley."

BIRTH OF THE NRA

At the outset of his administration President Roosevelt showed no desire to interfere in the relations between business and labor. He was hopeful that his initial relief programs and his reform policies to increase farm incomes would

provide the kick start the economy so badly needed. In other words, he was not contemplating a wide-ranging industrial recovery program along the lines of the farm program.

•

"…whatever it is, it will taste awfully good to the people of the Tennessee Valley."

•

However, Roosevelt soon came under pressure to address the predicament of industry both from within his own circle of advisers and from the Senate.

The dining hall at a Civilian Conservation Corps camp in California in 1933. Millions would eventually participate in the program.

There, a radical proposal put forward by Senator Hugo Black of Alabama was gaining support by the day. Black proposed cutting the working week to 30 hours, which would have the effect of sharing the national work load among more people—thereby slashing unemployment. He claimed that his program would create six million jobs.

Roosevelt was opposed to the scheme, which he thought too inflexible, and it made no mention of minimum wages. He felt that instead of spreading existing jobs more thinly, it made more sense, as he put it, to "create new

The Popular Program

Of all the New Deal programs the Civilian Conservation Corps was probably the most enduringly popular (it continued until 1942). There were several reasons for this. It was easy to understand the purpose of the program, and it was obviously effective as a relief measure. It brought much-needed business into the nearby towns that serviced the camps. And the tasks performed—restoration of historic sites, wildlife protection, the planting of millions of trees—were highly visible and of instinctive appeal to the public at large.

employment and to stimulate industrial confidence." But the Black proposal, which was passed by the Senate on April 6, 1933, put him on the spot to come up with something better.

Characteristically, Roosevelt set in train three competing groups to draft proposals for an industrial recovery act. Each group approached the subject from a different slant, and there were heated arguments as they attempted to hammer out a final draft together. Roosevelt became so impatient with the wrangling at one point that he told them to shut themselves in a room and stay there until they had thrashed out a bill they were all satisfied with. It would seem that what he wanted was a bill that had something for industry and something for labor, even if it contained contradictory elements.

The omnibus bill put before the House of Representatives therefore had something of a scattergun feel to it. To gain the support of businessmen, it provided backing for codes of fair competition, which were intended to prevent ruinous price-cutting. Labor was granted the right to collective bargaining, with guarantees of minimum wages and maximum hours of work (see Volume 4, Chapter 6, "The Unionization of Labor"). These provisions were to be administered by the National Recovery Administration (NRA). The bill also earmarked $3.3 billion for a public works program. It was to be administered by the Public Works Administration (PWA).

The House passed the bill by 325 votes to 76. It did not have such an easy ride in the Senate and was finally passed by only seven votes. On June 16, 1933, the last of the Hundred Days, the president signed the National Industrial Recovery Act into law.

THE CIVILIAN CONSERVATION CORPS

Among the general misery of mass unemployment one category of unemployed particularly disturbed Roosevelt. Joblessness was blighting the lives of the young,

Tree-cutting at a CCC camp in Sequoia National Park, California, in 1933. The CCC gained popular approval throughout its life.

disillusioning them at the outset of their adulthood. It was estimated that a quarter of a million young people were just drifting from place to place. Quite unrelated to that problem, Roosevelt had all his life been keenly committed to conservation. He planted thousands of trees at his home in Hyde Park; and when he was governor of New York, he organized 10,000 men to work on a reforestation program.

In the opening days of his presidency Roosevelt made an inspired connection between youth unemployment and the conservation of natural resources. Why not set the young to work on conservation programs? It would restore a sense of self-worth in the young men, as well as keeping them out of trouble. And it would do city-dwellers no harm at all to get out into the countryside and become involved in some worthwhile physical work.

On March 21, 1933, FDR launched the Civilian Conservation Corps (CCC). By its provisions 2,600 camps were set up to organize building dams, draining marshland and controlling floods, fighting forest fires, planting trees, and restoring beaches. The volunteers got their keep plus $30 a month, $25 of which was sent back to their families. The CCC camps were among the most visible signs of the New Deal and among its greatest successes. To remove young men from the dole and get them involved in healthy work while improving the landscape and safeguarding resources was a win-win policy.

END OF THE HUNDRED DAYS

On June 16, 1933, the 73rd Congress adjourned. In a little over three months it had passed 15 major acts, more legislation than any Congress in history. In consequence, the nation was on the road to recovery. It would be a rocky road, and twisting, but the darkest tunnel of the Depression seemed many miles behind. Roosevelt attended his son Franklin, Jr.'s, graduation from Groton school, and then went on a sailing holiday with his son James off the New England coast.

—— SEE ALSO ——

◆ Volume 2, Chapter 1,
The Election of 1932

◆ Volume 2, Chapter 3,
The Roosevelts: A New Style

◆ Volume 2, Chapter 4,
Where Did the Depression Bite?

◆ Volume 2, Chapter 5,
Putting People to Work

◆ Volume 3, Chapter 1,
Tough in the City

◆ Volume 3, Chapter 2,
Shadow over the Countryside

◆ Volume 4, Chapter 2,
The Supreme Court

The Age of the Acronym

A memorable feature of the New Deal was the way the bewildering array of government measures and agencies was reduced to an equally bewildering series of abbreviations or acronyms. As a consequence they were sometimes referred to as a group as the "alphabet agencies." As though in imitation, it became commonplace in the United States wherever possible to apply supposedly memorable acronyms to other organizations—from pressure groups to industrial giants. Here is a sample of what Americans in the 1930s would have regularly encountered; some of these acronyms remain very familiar at the beginning of the 21st century.

AAA	Agricultural Adjustment Administration
ACPF	American Commonwealth Political Federation
ADA	Americans for Democratic Action
ADC	Aid to Dependent Children
AFL	American Federation of Labor
AMA	American Medical Association
BAC	Business Advisory Council
BAE	Bureau of Agricultural Economics
CAWIU	Cannery and Agricultural Workers Industrial Union
CCC	Civilian Conservation Corps
CIO	Committee for (later Congress of) Industrial Organization
CWA	Civil Works Administration
ERA	Equal Rights Amendment
FAP	Federal Art Project
FERA	Federal Emergency Relief Administration
FHA	Farmers' Holiday Association
FHA	Federal Housing Administration
FRB	Federal Reserve Board
FSA	Farm Security Administration
GE	General Electric
GM	General Motors
ILGWU	International Ladies' Garment Workers' Union
LIPA	League for Independent Political Action

MWIU	Maritime Workers International Union
NAACP	National Association for the Advancement of Colored People
NAM	National Association of Manufacturers
NIRA	National Industrial Recovery Act
NLB	National Labor Board
NLRB	National Labor Relations Board
NRA	National Recovery Administration
NWLB	National War Labor Board
NYA	National Youth Administration
POUR	President's Organization for Unemployment Relief
PWA	Public Works Administration
PWAP	Public Works Art Project
RA	Resettlement Administration
REA	Rural Electrification Administration
RFC	Reconstruction Finance Corporation
SCS	Soil Conservation Service
SEC	Securities and Exchange Commission
STFU	Southern Tenant Farmers' Union
SWOC	Steel Workers' Organizing Committee
TERA	Temporary Emergency Relief Administration
TNEC	Temporary National Economic Committee
TVA	Tennessee Valley Authority
UAW	United Automobile Workers
UE	United Electrical, Radio and Machine Workers
UMW	United Mine Workers
URW	United Rubber Workers
USHA	United States Housing Authority
UTW	United Textile Workers
WIB	War Industries Board
WPA	Works Progress Administration

3

THE ROOSEVELTS: A NEW STYLE

The 32nd president of the United States and his First Lady brought a refreshing tone to the White House. For not only was FDR a visibly genial man, both he and Eleanor, from greatly privileged backgrounds themselves, conveyed a genuine sympathy with the sufferings of the American people.

The Roosevelts on a Washington-bound train in 1935, midway through the first term of FDR's record tenure in the White House.

The Roosevelts entered the White House on March 4, 1933, on a wave of public expectation (see Chapter 1, "The Election of 1932"). Not since Abraham Lincoln had assumed the presidency in 1861, when the United States faced imminent breakup, had a new president come into office with the nation in such a desperate plight.

While it was not at all clear to the American people what their new leader would do to tackle the crisis, there were clues to his character in the way he presented himself to them. Whereas his predecessor, Herbert Hoover, had appeared ever glummer and more withdrawn as the economy spiraled out of control, Roosevelt was a conspicuously upbeat and optimistic fellow, forever smiling and prone to laughing in public. In fact, he was the first president to go out of his way to smile when engaged in public duties. He had two other trademark gestures by which the public came to recognize

Franklin in Highland garb with his doting mother in 1887. She seemed certain from the time of his birth that he would achieve greatness.

of someone who was actually on their side. And so they adored him in a way that no president before or since has ever been so adored by so many from so many different stations in life.

1. A GILDED YOUTH

Franklin Delano Roosevelt was born on January 30, 1882, to James Roosevelt (1828–1900) and Sara Delano Roosevelt (1854–1941), the latter once being described as not so much a woman as a social presence. A member of the blue-blooded Delano family, she could boast of 13 ancestral links with the Pilgrim Fathers and the *Mayflower*. Even by the standards of upper-class Americans at the time she was breathtakingly grand and imperious in her manner. Social equals (of whom she admitted few) went in fear of the great lady, including her beloved son, whose life she tried to control long into his adulthood.

James Roosevelt was an equally prominent member of the

him: the rimless glasses clipped on the bridge of his nose and the cigarette holder clamped between his teeth and usually tilted upward at a jaunty angle.

To his enemies Roosevelt's geniality and all such behavioral tics were just affectations and showmanship, revealing Roosevelt's shallowness and lack of scruple. But to the vast numbers of men and women who looked to Roosevelt to take a lead, from the earliest days and throughout his long tenure in office, the smiling man in the White House was uncannily like a personal friend. To

The Roosevelt family at their Hyde Park estate during Franklin's privileged childhood, when he was educated at home by tutors.

them the friendly grin, the twinkling eyes, the sonorous voice on the radio signaled that the highest office in the land was in the hands

A serious-looking Franklin at the age of 12, posing with his father, then in his late 60s and easily old enough to be the boy's grandfather.

landed gentry, descended from Klaes Van Roosevelt, who owned property in old New Amsterdam from the 1640s. Theodore Roosevelt (1858–1919; see Volume 1, Chapter 1, "The United States, 1865–1914") too was a direct descendant of Klaes Van Roosevelt, which made the two presidents fifth cousins. James Roosevelt had business interests in coal and railroads, but his real passion was for his country estate, Springwood, at Hyde Park on the Hudson River. At Franklin's birth Sara was 26, and James, a widower when he married her, was 53.

This, then, was the world of wealth and privilege into which

Franklin Delano Roosevelt was born. He was an only child, pampered and indulged especially by a mother who believed from his infancy that he was destined for greatness. The self-centeredness of Franklin's childhood might have created a character of a stultifying selfishness. Instead, he acquired a trait often associated with only children reared by doting parents. He had unshakable self-assurance, a quality that would become one of his defining characteristics in life.

HYDE PARK DAYS

Franklin was educated by tutors at the Hyde Park estate until the age of 14. His education was under his

The proud young photographer, himself photographed at the Delano home in Fairhaven, Mass., in 1897, soon after his enrollment at Groton.

mother's supervision, and it has been said that he may have developed an early skill at manipulation in the process of trying to please her. His actual education was carried out by a succession of governesses and private tutors, and from the age of three he accompanied his parents on their yearly trip to Europe. He learned to speak and write German and French, and at the age of nine attended a private school for six weeks where, his mother thought, he would improve his German. While she pampered him, his mother also controlled him with firmness, insisting on a rigid schedule with specific times for various activities during the day. She persisted with this sort of behavior long into his adulthood, for example, insisting that he put on galoshes before going outdoors on a rainy day.

Early in his youth Franklin became interested in birds; and

when he was given a gun for his eleventh birthday, he set out to collect a specimen of every species of bird in his native Dutchess County. By the time he entered college, he had collected and identified over 300 different species. His collection remains one of the most comprehensive from that county. He learned how to stuff and mount the birds himself, then gave the job to a taxidermist. Warren Delano, his grandfather, was so taken by the boy's interest in and knowledge of birds that he gave Franklin a life membership in the American Museum of Natural History. Franklin spent many hours there looking at the exhibits and attending lectures.

As the future heir to the Hyde Park estate, Franklin's interest in nature and natural history would serve him well. All his life he retained a huge affection for the estate and considered himself to be a man of the country, not the city. He later said, "I never have been and I hope I never will be, a resident of New York City." As president, when discussing agricultural matters and the plight of the farming community, he would invariably describe himself as a fellow farmer. What he was, of course, was a gentleman farmer in the tradition of the English landed gentry, with 175 people dependent on the estate. He fell into the habit of addressing the people on the estate by their first names (almost unheard of at the time), and he later found that this worked to his advantage in politics, where such informality reinforced the impression he so strongly conveyed of being comfortable with people of all backgrounds. It has been said

Franklin, second from left in the bottom row, as a member of the Groton School football team in 1899, his final year.

that it was Roosevelt who instigated the modern American custom of addressing people by their first names after just a brief acquaintance.

To Groton and Harvard
At the age of 14 Franklin was sent away to Groton School, a prestigious preparatory school in Groton, Massachusetts, where he studied under the celebrated educator Endicott Peabody and gained a solid education. He did well, earning good grades, but was considered shy and had few close friends. The young Roosevelt was often thought to have an English accent and used phrases such as

A Lasting Influence

Endicott Peabody, who founded Groton School 35 miles northwest of Boston in 1884 and ran it with absolute commitment for 56 years, made an enduring impression on Franklin Roosevelt. Peabody believed deeply that boys from privileged families should get involved in politics rather than simply amass wealth, as had become the custom in the United States. Few of his students heeded Peabody's plea, but his words were not lost on the young FDR, who later said, "As long as I live, the influence of Dr. and Mrs. Peabody means and will mean more to me than that of any other people next to my father and mother."

"it's not cricket," although he never played the game.

Franklin left Groton in 1900 and enrolled that year at Harvard University. He majored in history but did not distinguish himself academically. However, he joined the intramural rowing and football teams, and enjoyed himself as secretary of the Freshman Glee Club. In 1903 he was appointed editor of the Harvard *Crimson*, the university newspaper, where he found it easier to make friends. He was also elected to the Hasty Pudding Club, whose oath displayed an unashamed elitism typical of the time and place. "Resolved: that the Lord's anointed shall inherit the Earth. Resolved: that we are the Lord's anointed."

2. POLITICS AND MARRIAGE

It was fashionable among the American upper classes of the time to consider politics beneath them, since in a democracy electioneering necessarily involved appealing to the lower classes for their support. James Roosevelt, who held such a view, repeatedly refused to run for office and even declined an appointment from President Grover Cleveland in 1885, since it would have entailed lengthy absences from his beloved Hyde Park.

Franklin Roosevelt, however, like his older cousin Theodore, drew the exact opposite conclusion about the appropriateness of politics as an activity for a gentleman. Like the Founding Fathers, they took for granted that with privileges of wealth and position came obligations to the wider community. And politics was a natural expression of the urge to become involved in public service.

In 1904 Franklin entered Columbia University Law School, the law being seen then as now as a natural grounding for a career in politics. He passed the bar examination in 1907 and went to work as a clerk for a law firm in New York City, where he remained for the next three years. He had no enthusiasm for the law and was using it as a stepping stone to a political career. The fact that his cousin had now been president for six years made his entry into politics effortless, even though it was for the Democratic Party rather than the president's Republicans. Both the Delanos and James Roosevelt's branch of the family were Democrats by long tradition, so Franklin Roosevelt could be said to have been a Democrat by birth as well as by inclination or political conviction.

STATE SENATOR

FDR's political career began when he accepted an invitation from the state Democratic leaders to run for the New York senate. They favored him for his obvious name recognition, and also because as a man of independent means he might be expected to pay his own election expenses. Although he accepted, he did so with no great expectation of winning. The Republicans had for 50 years controlled the district he was aiming to represent. Despite any such reservations, however, Roosevelt threw himself into

●

"Resolved: that we are the Lord's anointed."

●

the fray with characteristic enthusiasm. He ran on a ticket calling for clean government and declaring his opposition to "big-city bosses," a reference to the widespread corruption in city politics, not least in New York City. Roosevelt won the election and entered the New York senate at 29 years of age.

Clashing with Tammany Hall

The young senator quickly made a name for himself as a skillful political fighter who stood by his beliefs and was not under the thumb of Tammany Hall, a name that was infamous in New York politics during the late 19th and early 20th centuries. Tammany Hall was the name by which the Tammany Society became known because that was the society's headquarters at 331 Madison Avenue. The Tammany Society originated as a "fraternity of patriots consecrated to the independence, the popular liberty, and the federal union of the country." It soon became involved in politics, emerging as the Democratic Party machine in New York City and New York State. Roosevelt showed his independent-mindedness when he led a group of Democratic legislators in a successful revolt against a candidate chosen by Tammany Hall for the U.S. Senate. This did not sit well with Tammany Hall, particularly since it was eyeing him as good material for the party machine. Instead, Roosevelt became known as the leader of the anti-Tammany Democrats.

Roosevelt's brush with Tammany Hall had early consequences when in 1914 he sought the Democratic nomination as a candidate for the U.S. Senate. He lost by a wide margin, chiefly because Tammany Hall opposed him. This was not the last time that Roosevelt and Tammany Hall would square off with one another.

ELEANOR'S YOUTH

Anna Eleanor Roosevelt was born in New York City on October 11, 1884, to Elliot and Anna Hall Roosevelt. Anna Hall was yet another glamorous member of the Hudson Valley gentry and a society beauty. Elliot Roosevelt was the younger brother of Theodore Roosevelt and was considered handsome and dashing, if lacking almost entirely in his famous brother's abundant drive and energy.

Allenswood School in a leafy London suburb in 1900. Here Eleanor enjoyed herself and gained much-needed confidence after her difficult, lonely childhood.

Eleanor Roosevelt's official debutante photograph, in 1902. She began receiving her cousin Franklin's attentions soon after.

Eleanor, however, did not inherit her parents' good looks. She saw herself as plain and often sensed that her mother was disappointed that she was not prettier. "She is such a funny child," her mother would say, "so old-fashioned that we always call her granny." Eleanor recalls that her mother "tried very hard to bring me up well so my manners would in some way compensate for my looks, but her efforts only made me more keenly conscious of my shortcomings." It is little wonder that she became shy, withdrawn, and fearful. The child only came out of herself in the presence of her father, who called her his "Little Nell" and lavished affection on her. Unfortunately this paternal love, which she craved, was all too sporadic because Elliot Roosevelt was a chronic alcoholic. As his condition worsened, much of his time was divided between drinking binges and fruitless stays in clinics searching for a cure from his addiction.

The bride in her wedding dress in 1905. Tall, willowy, and with a rich mane of dark hair, she presented a strikingly attractive figure.

extraordinary 70-year-old French-woman, Marie Souvestre, who was a political free-thinker and a professed atheist. "Sou," as she was affectionately known, introduced Eleanor to an entirely new world, and the young American girl took to it with enthusiasm, later describing her three years at Allenswood as the happiest of her life. She was singled out for special attention by Sou because of her eagerness to learn and also because she behaved with poise in company. Eleanor accompanied her mentor to Italy on vacation, which further broadened the horizons of the girl who had felt shut out of life. The effect of this European experience in her life

was to rid Eleanor of her inhibitions and fears and to make her a composed young woman.

When she returned to the United States at 18 years of age, she went through her debutante season, marking her formal entry into society. She did not enjoy

•

"Why me? I am plain. I have nothing to bring you."

•

"coming out" much, however, and reproached herself yet again for falling short of her mother's glamorous example. Of more lasting significance, however, she began taking an interest in social work,

Her health perhaps broken by coping with such a husband, Anna Hall Roosevelt died when Eleanor was eight years old. Two years later, at the age of 34, Elliot Roosevelt died as the result of a drunken fall. Eleanor went with her two brothers to live with her maternal grandmother, Mrs. Valentine Hall, a rich New York widow who had also been a society beauty. She held the belief that "no" was always easier to say than "yes" and brought the children up under strict discipline. The governess who looked after them adhered to the same unyielding regime.

At 15 Eleanor was sent to a finishing school in the suburbs of London, England, called Allenswood. The school was run by an

The proud parents of toddler Anna and baby James in 1908. The young family man was now about to make his entrance on the political stage.

which would become a lifelong commitment of Eleanor Roosevelt's in one form or another.

Courtship and marriage

It was at this time that Eleanor came to the attention of her distant cousin, the handsome young Franklin Delano Roosevelt. They became friends, and he became her regular companion. When Franklin first proposed to her, on a trip to Massachusetts, she apparently replied, "Why me? I am plain, I have nothing to bring you." But Franklin obviously thought otherwise, and it was noted at the time that while she was not a beauty, she was certainly attractive to men. He persisted, and in 1903 the couple became engaged.

Sara Roosevelt, when informed of this development, took no trouble to disguise her displeasure. She did not want another woman in her precious son's life and used all her considerable influence to thwart the union. She went so far as to take him on a Caribbean cruise in the hope that its pleasures might cause him to forget Eleanor. For once the formidable Sara Roosevelt did not get her way, and the marriage went ahead in 1905. But she made clear that she was going to remain a factor in the young couple's life. While they were on their honeymoon in Europe, she rented for their return a house in Manhattan, three blocks from her own town house, and furnished it completely to her own taste. Eleanor accepted this *fait accompli* rather than provoke a quarrel with her mother-in-law, and this was to become a settled pattern. Eleanor accepted Sara's

The assistant secretary of the Navy climbs the rigging on a naval vessel. Roosevelt had a lifelong love of boats and sailing.

interference with stoicism all her life while simply getting on with things herself.

The Roosevelts had six children. They were Anna Eleanor (1906–1975); James (1907–1991); Franklin Delano, Jr. (died in infancy, 1909); Elliott (1910–1990); Franklin Delano, Jr. (1914–1988); and John (1916–1981). James and Franklin, Jr., both served in the United States House of Representatives.

The Roosevelt's marriage came under great strain when in 1918 Eleanor discovered that her husband had for some time been conducting an affair with her personal secretary, Lucy Mercer. While she held back from divorce, which would have damaged if not

ruined her husband's political career, Eleanor Roosevelt permanently ended marital relations with her husband from that time. Their marriage would be held together, however, by their shared political beliefs and by Eleanor's realization that her husband's glittering political prospects held out the chance for both of them to achieve great goals.

ASSISTANT SECRETARY OF THE NAVY

In 1912 Theodore Roosevelt came out of retirement to run again for the presidency. Despite the fact that Franklin both liked and greatly admired his famous cousin, his loyalty to the Democratic Party came first, and he supported

Assistant Secretary of the Navy Roosevelt addressing a rally for the Victory Loan drive from the steps of the Navy Department in 1919.

Woodrow Wilson. When Wilson won the election, he appointed Franklin assistant secretary of the Navy. Roosevelt was more than pleased with his new post. He said, "I now find my vocation combined with my avocation in a delightful way." His vocation, of course, was his commitment to politics, while his avocation (hobby) was ships and naval history, which had been a consuming interest from childhood days.

Roosevelt worked directly under Josephus Daniels (1862–1948), the secretary of the Navy. Daniels was more than a navy man or politician, however; he was essentially a newspaperman and editor. He was born in Washington, North Carolina, and educated at the University of North Carolina. He began newspaper work in the

town of Wilson, North Carolina. One of his achievements was to consolidate the *State Chronicle* and the *North Carolinian* to form the *Raleigh News and Observer*. He edited it from 1894 until his death. In the meantime he served as secretary of the Navy from 1913 to 1921 and as ambassador to Mexico from 1933 to 1942.

Daniels was an old hand at the political game and passed on his knowledge to the young Roosevelt. He especially made sure that Roosevelt knew how to deal with Congress. Later, when the United States had entered World War I, Roosevelt wanted to enter military service, but Daniels persuaded him to remain at his desk. This gave Roosevelt the opportunity to work on important wartime projects, including the laying of antisubmarine mines in the North Sea. This was to benefit his future political career since he gained a reputation for getting things done. It also gave him the chance to tour European

battlefields after the war, which raised his public profile. People began to take notice of him and to warm to his style and personality.

VICE-PRESIDENTIAL CANDIDATE

For the 1920 presidential elections the Democratic National Convention chose Governor James M. Cox (1870–1957) of Ohio as its presidential nominee. Since Ohio was a Midwestern state, the delegates wanted a vice-presidential candidate from an eastern state to balance the ticket. The convention nominated Roosevelt, at 38 the youngest vice-presidential candidate there had been. Cox and Roosevelt campaigned vigorously on a platform that called for United States membership in the League of Nations, which was largely the creation of the outgoing president, Woodrow Wilson. Wilson, however, who was desperately ill following a stroke, had failed to convince either the Senate or the American people of the case for participating in the League (see Volume 1, Chapter 3, "The Return to Normalcy"). Cox and Roosevelt were easily defeated, and Republican Warren G. Harding became president. The defeat probably did Roosevelt no harm. His public profile was enlarged, and he established himself as a leader among progressive Democrats. There was plenty of time for his political career to resume its smooth progress. That year he became a vice-president of the Fidelity and Deposit Company of Maryland, a surety and bond company, taking charge of its New York branch.

3. OVERCOMING AFFLICTION

The Roosevelt family liked to spend part of the summer at their vacation home on Campobello

Georgia Warm Springs Foundation

Roosevelt did as much as he could to reduce the effects of his paralysis. He regained the use of his hands and his back. He exercised regularly and developed great upper-body strength. He used the gymnasium often and began to work on his legs. He suffered several falls and made a little progress, but he was never able to walk again without help or braces on his legs.

Swimming was an exercise that Roosevelt indulged in despite the fact that a water-borne virus had apparently caused the paralysis. Swimming gave him a chance to exercise his legs, and in 1924 Roosevelt began to spend time at the mineral water spa at Warm Springs, Georgia. The waters had been known to help other polio victims, so he thought they might help him. There he met people who could barely afford the cost of polio treatment. The

following year, with a group of friends, Roosevelt established the Georgia Warm Springs Foundation, which offered low-cost treatment for fellow "polios," as Roosevelt affectionately called other sufferers. The Warm Springs Foundation inspired the March of Dimes program, which funded the research that eventually found a vaccine for polio.

Roosevelt by the pool at Warm Springs, where he conducted exercise programs for fellow polio victims; they called him "Dr. Roosevelt."

Island off the coast of New Brunswick in Canada. On August 4, 1921, Roosevelt went sailing and while doing so fell into the water. The next day, he recalled, he felt tired and went for a swim in order to refresh himself. Later he wrote, "I didn't feel the same reaction. When I reached the house, the mail was in, with several newspapers I hadn't seen. I sat reading for a while, too tired even to dress." The next day he felt worse. "My left leg lagged," he recalled. "Presently it refused to work, and then the other."

After three days Roosevelt could not stand on either leg. His back, arms, and hands became partially paralyzed, and he could

not hold a pen to write. These were classic symptoms of polio, or infantile paralysis as it was called at the time, and indeed that dread diagnosis was soon confirmed, although it was hoped the attack would turn out to be a mild one. However, for all his natural optimism Roosevelt had an ominous feeling about his condition. "While the doctors were unanimous in telling me that the attack was very mild...I had the usual dark suspicion that they were just saying nice things to make me feel good." His suspicions were confirmed, and later, while in bed in New York City, he was careful to show his children his withered legs, telling them how the disease had affected

him so that they would understand his situation.

In January of the following year his condition became worse. He remained in good spirits, however; and when his old boss Josephus Daniels came to visit, he hit him on the chest so hard it made the man stagger. Roosevelt laughed and said, "You thought you were coming to see an invalid, but I can knock you out in any bout."

Roosevelt's obstinacy in not allowing the disease to dampen his spirits in public would stand him in good stead when he reemerged into the political arena. Critically, rather than viewing him as a man weakened by his condition, which would have been politically

The Illusion of Walking

For all the effort Roosevelt put into recovering the use of his legs, the polio attack left him permanently paralyzed from the waist down. Yet people did not really picture him like that because he trained himself to "walk" in public with crutches and leg braces. Furthermore, press photographers and newsreel cameramen obeyed a gentlemen's agreement not to portray the president as an invalid. So the image conveyed to the public was of FDR seated or standing (clenching an aide's arm), not confined to a wheelchair.

fatal, people came to see him as a man of strength and courage, capable of overturning the odds and succeeding where weaker men might fail.

RETURN TO POLITICS

Sara Roosevelt hoped that polio would end her son's political ambitions, and that he would retire to the life of a country gentleman. Many others thought that Roosevelt would follow his mother's wishes. But he refused to listen. He continued his political activity by writing letters, issuing statements, and holding conferences in his home, helped and encouraged by his wife and his loyal aide, Louis M. Howe (1871–1936).

A Famous Speech

Roosevelt finally made his public return to politics in 1924. It was a spectacular and dramatic moment as, amid thundering applause, he appeared on crutches to nominate Governor Alfred E. Smith (1873–1944) of New York for president at the Democratic National Convention. Smith lost the nomination to John W. Davis because of splits in the party over Prohibition and the Ku Klux Klan: Smith opposed both at a time when they had much support, and was also a Catholic in a mainly Protestant nation. The nominating speech, however, greatly boosted Roosevelt's image and gained him ever more supporters within the party.

In 1928 Roosevelt again helped Smith, who won the Democratic nomination for president this time. Smith in turn arranged for Roosevelt's nomination to succeed him as governor of New York. Smith lost the presidential election, but Roosevelt was narrowly elected governor of New York.

GOVERNOR OF NEW YORK

As governor of New York Roosevelt initiated much progressive legislation, and his vigorous response to the onset of the Great Depression provided a foretaste of what was to come. He established the country's first system of relief for the unemployed in New York and brought about tighter control of utilities among other things. Such efforts were noted and widely approved, and Roosevelt was reelected by a much larger majority in 1930. He was now widely seen as a leading contender for the presidential nomination in 1932. Eleanor Roosevelt was in two minds about this since, naturally, she knew better than anyone what a great physical liability her husband labored

Roosevelt is helped from a car in the late 1930s: Few Americans got to see such revealing pictures of the extent of the president's disability.

under, but she also knew how tough he was. As she once expressed it, "If polio did not kill him, the presidency won't." She willingly assisted writers who were preparing Roosevelt biographies, and she worked diligently in the Women's Division of the Democratic Party. She also researched material for her husband's speeches and began to fulfill the role of her immobilized husband's eyes and ears, a service that she would continue to provide for the rest of his life.

4. THE ROAD TO THE WHITE HOUSE

The widespread recognition and respect Roosevelt had gained from his years as governor of New York, his amiable disposition, and his willingness to tackle problems were increasingly seen in sharp contrast with Hoover's dour disposition and his apparent inability to solve any of the problems crippling the nation. These qualities made Roosevelt an ideal candidate for the Democrats. In April 1932 he struck a deep chord when in a nationwide radio address he outlined a program to meet the economic crisis gripping the nation. Recovery, he said, had to be built around the average American, whom Roosevelt described as the "forgotten man."

While Roosevelt was by now considered a certainty in the forthcoming presidential election, he still had to receive the Democratic nomination, and he had enemies within the party, not least Tammany Hall, determined to keep him from getting it. But in July 1932 in Chicago, on the fourth ballot, Roosevelt finally gained the required majority for the nomination. He immediately flew from Albany to Chicago to accept the nomination, another imaginative gesture at a time when air travel was a novelty. This was the first time a presidential nominee had made an acceptance speech at the national convention; the practice would become routine after FDR's example.

In his speech he promised a "new deal" to lead the nation out of its economic doldrums. It was a clever piece of "sound-bite" poli-

The Roosevelts shortly after moving into the White House in 1933, as the culmination of FDR's masterful political campaign.

tics, and it provided a slogan not just for the election but also a phrase to encapsulate the dynamic early phase of his presidency.

On the campaign trail FDR visited 38 states and in doing so convinced voters that his physical fitness was not an issue. His campaign song was the cheery "Happy Days Are Here Again"; and if people were hardly able to believe that fantasy, there was much in Roosevelt's confident manner that convinced them that there might at least be better days ahead with him in the White House. On November 8, 1932, they sent him to the White House with a massive vote of confidence.

A fireside chat in 1935, the president flanked by the network radio microphones that carried his voice into millions of homes.

THE PRESIDENT IN ACTION

Eight days after his inauguration on March 4, 1933, the new president used the radio to tell the people about the banking crisis and what he intended to do about it. He wanted to make sure Americans knew what was going on, thereby beginning to restore some confidence in the government, which had taken such a battering under his predecessor. No president before had had the means or perhaps the desire to get this close to the people. Roosevelt instinctively related to people in a friendly, apparently informal way, as though he and they were on a first-name basis. It was radical and made possible only by the radio technology available. So began FDR's famous Sunday evening "fireside chats," a regular updating on the state of affairs as

he perceived it, a sort of presidential progress report. In these radio broadcasts FDR displayed presentational skills of an exceptional order, and his vast radio audience hung on every word. And they believed him.

In the first fireside chat he explained that all the banks that were sound would reopen the following day and thanks to his Emergency Banking Act would be safe. When the banks opened the next morning, there was no stampede to withdraw funds, and by the end of that day bank deposits exceeded withdrawals. In that moment the American banking system, which had been poised to collapse only a few days earlier, was saved. Such was the difference caused by confidence in the new president, with his reassuring message and manner.

A domestic scene as Eleanor Roosevelt takes her dog for a walk in May 1933, at the outset of the White House years.

wise and sensible beginning has been made. In the present spirit of mutual confidence and mutual encouragement we go forward."

A Whirlwind of Activity

Roosevelt's dynamic style involved swift action. He partly blamed the Depression on the preceding administration's failure to take proper measures and the insistence of its leaders to work in "the pattern of an outworn tradition." Swiftness, boldness, and courage would save the country, he maintained, so he plunged into a frenzy

•

"In the present spirit of mutual confidence... we go forward."

•

of activity in the opening days of his administration. In the "first hundred days," as historian Arthur M. Schlesinger, Jr., noted, he "sent 15 messages to Congress, guided 15 major laws to enactment, delivered 10 speeches, held press conferences and cabinet meetings twice a week, conducted talks with foreign heads of state, made all the decisions in domestic and foreign policy..." (see Chapter 2, "The First Hundred Days"). He went on to create a multitude of acts and authorities from the Emergency Banking Act to the Farm Credit Act, and from the Civilian Conservation Corps to the Tennessee Valley Authority (see Chapter 5,

On May 7, 1933, Roosevelt began the second of his chats in the now-familiar warm and relaxed tone: "On a Sunday night a week after my inauguration I used the radio to tell you about the banking crisis and the measures we were taking to meet it.... Tonight, eight weeks later, I come for the second time to give you my report—in the same spirit and by the same means to tell you about what we have been doing and what we are planning to do." He went on to give a pledge to justify the confidence they had placed in both him and his government. He ended the report, "To you, the people of this country, all of us, the members of the Congress and members of this administration owe a profound debt of gratitude. Throughout the Depression you have been patient. You have granted us wide powers, you have encouraged us with widespread approval of our purposes. Every ounce of strength and every resource at our command we have devoted to the end of justifying your confidence. We are encouraged to believe that a

Independent-minded First Lady

Some weeks after FDR's victory in 1932, Eleanor Roosevelt was contacted by the outgoing president's wife, Mrs. Lou Hoover, who offered to show the First Lady-elect around the White House. After agreeing on a morning for the visit, Mrs. Hoover enquired as to where she should send the White House limousine and the military aide to pick up Mrs. Roosevelt. To her consternation her successor refused both the car and the aide. She planned, she said, to walk over from the Mayflower Hotel after breakfast.

The State Department's chief of protocol, a family relation, was horrified when he heard of the plan. "But Eleanor, darling," he cried, "you can't do that. People will recognize you. You'll be mobbed." The protest went unheeded. When it was time to make the tour, Mrs. Roosevelt, with a friend, walked over to the White House, and after the tour of her future home returned on foot to the Mayflower Hotel. Neither the White House staff nor Mrs. Hoover quite got over it.

Eleanor Roosevelt, as much as her husband, had a natural instinct for ignoring trivial conventions. When in the White House her style did not change. She insisted, for instance, on operating the White House elevator herself instead of having the chief usher operate it for her. Most significantly, though, soon after FDR's inauguration she began holding press conferences of her own for the women reporters.

"Washington has never seen the like," wrote Bess Furman in a story about Mrs. Roosevelt for the Associated Press. "A social transformation has taken place with the New Deal." Indeed it had. With the arrival of the Roosevelts the White House as well as the United States entered a time of transition.

The First Lady on a visit to Maine in 1941. Never before had a president's wife taken such an active part in the nation's political life.

"Putting People to Work"). Judged individually, some of these measures were very successful and others much less so. But the very fact of this whirlwind of activity showed how determined the new administration was to tackle the Depression head on rather than wait for the economy to right itself. The contrast between this activism and the hand-wringing inaction that had gone before was striking (see Volume 4, Chapter 1, "Left vs. Right"). There was simply no precedent for the New Deal, no model for a president who was prepared to try practically anything in his effort to get the nation on its feet. And when one of the new plans was proven not to work, Roosevelt simply scrapped it without the slightest embarrassment and tried something different in its place.

A beaming First Lady with the charges of a Works Progress Administration nursery school in Des Moines, Iowa, in 1936.

THE FIRST LADY

Eleanor Roosevelt did not look forward to life in the White House. She was apprehensive of the endless round of ceremonies and entertaining that would effectively imprison her. Her fears were unfounded, however, as she realized how great the opportunities were to help her husband and to serve the public. While the Roosevelts were in Albany, an editor of the *Nashville Tennessean*

did a piece on her life as the governor's wife and predicted that she would cause a greater stir in Washington than Theodore Roosevelt's vivacious daughter Alice had done in the early years of the century. "It begins to look as if Anna Eleanor Roosevelt is going to make Alice Roosevelt Longworth look like Alice-sit-by-the-fire," wrote the editor. It was a shrewd prediction; and although the First Lady was perfectly competent at presiding over teas, receptions, state dinners, and the like, it was her political agenda and the way she became so influential in the policies and

programs of her husband that marked her out as a rare presidential wife.

A Political Force

Mrs. Roosevelt made a point of inspecting Washington's slums, which she reported to the press and to Congress, urging that they be cleaned up. She involved herself with New Deal programs and made useful suggestions for them when she could. In the NRA codes she insisted on consumer representation and equal pay for women. She persuaded AAA officials to use surplus farm foods to feed the hungry instead of destroying them in order to boost prices through scarcity. She also held frequent talks with CWA administrator Harry Hopkins (1890–1946) on work projects for the unemployed, especially women and children, and managed to get projects for unemployed writers, painters, actors, and musicians included in the program.

Woman of Letters

Eleanor Roosevelt was often besieged with letters. In 1933 she received no fewer than 300,000 of them. Some were extremely hurtful, but most were full of praise for what she was doing, both for women and for young people. Many were simply pleas for help. Again she dispensed with precedent by not relying on form letters. She took all of her letters seriously except the most venomous hate letters, which in any case were usually anonymous. Her staff sorted the letters and classified them so that they could be dealt with appropriately. Appeals for jobs, for instance, would be forwarded to the correct department. Eleanor also tried to find ways of responding to requests for money, although that was not

The NYA and Racial Justice

Eleanor Roosevelt was particularly anxious that young people who were out of work should be offered assistance under the New Deal. So in 1935 she conceived the idea of and helped develop the National Youth Administration, or NYA. The project was set up to provide employment for young people out of work and to give high school and college students part-time jobs so that they could continue with their education. Such was Mrs. Roosevelt's close personal involvement in the scheme that *Life* magazine reported that she "functions as a kind of inspector-general of the NYA project."

When the NYA was in its infancy, Mrs. Roosevelt asked that the black educator Mary McLeod Bethune (1875–1955) be placed on the advisory board to make sure that young blacks were given the opportunity to participate in the program (see Volume 5, Chapter 2, "Equality for Some"). The First Lady had not always been sympathetic to the problems of blacks; but by the time she got to the White House, the attitudes she had been brought up with in regard to race had changed, and she had developed considerable sympathy for the people often referred to as America's second-class citizens. She began to champion their causes and became a friend of Walter White, leader of the National Association for the Advancement of Colored People (NAACP).

Eleanor held talks frequently with both White and Mary McLeod Bethune about how blacks might be aided under the New Deal. She made sure that she entertained blacks as well as whites at the White House. She tried to persuade her husband to back an anti-lynching bill as well as a move to abolish the poll tax in Southern states that effectively disenfranchised black voters. FDR did not publicly support either measure, but on the other hand he did not discourage his wife from supporting them. Many of his close associates did not like it, however. Southern Democrats were almost all staunch supporters of racial segregation, and they formed an important part of FDR's political support.

In 1939 Eleanor Roosevelt attended the organizational meeting of the Southern Conference on Human Welfare in Birmingham, Alabama. The conference was open to both black and white delegates; but when Eleanor arrived, she found that blacks and whites were separated, blacks on one side of a central aisle and whites on the other. In a silent but unmistakable gesture of protest as the meeting proceeded, she slid her chair into the middle of the aisle separating the two races.

In 1939, when the Daughters of the American Revolution refused to allow the internationally celebrated black singer Marian Anderson to perform at Constitution Hall, the only place in Washington considered large enough to accommodate the anticipated crowds, Mrs. Roosevelt resigned from the DAR. Then she helped arrange an outdoor concert for the singer, which was performed on the steps of the Lincoln Memorial.

Eleanor Roosevelt speaking at the White House in March 1937, when she held an Easter party for more than 50,000 children.

easy. The most informative letters she answered personally, while passing some to the president. Some of the correspondence, though, was distinctly odd. One woman wrote to say that she wanted to adopt a baby and asked Mrs. Roosevelt to find one for her. She wrote again to say that when she had the baby, she would need a cow and then an ice-box for the milk.

Along with dealing with her massive correspondence, Eleanor Roosevelt gave much of her time to writing. She had begun contributing to magazines in the 1920s and was a competent journalist. Her new responsibilities in the White House did not curb her journalistic output. She just worked harder. In 1934 she began writing a monthly column for the *Woman's Home Companion* magazine. It was entitled "Mrs. Roosevelt's Page" and ranged in subject matter from education to garden-

ing, from recreation to old age. She went on to write a newspaper column called "My Day" and in time published a number of books.

An Enduring Legacy

Eleanor Roosevelt became one of the best-loved figures in America, admired by the poor and the well-to-do alike. Adlai Stevenson, twice unsuccessful Democratic presidential candidate in the 1950s, said of her, "What other single human being has touched and transformed the existence of so many? She walked in the slums and ghettos of the world, not on a tour of inspection, but as one who could not feel contentment when others were hungry."

THE FDR TOUCH

When Roosevelt gave his inaugural address on March 4, 1933, he emphasized the need for a new style of government in the United States, stating that his accession

The great contralto Marian Anderson in concert at the Lincoln Memorial in April 1939, an event Mrs. Roosevelt helped organize.

A Working Widow

FDR's death in 1945 did not curtail Eleanor Roosevelt's long career as a champion of liberal causes. Her activities took on a global dimension when she was appointed as a delegate to the United Nations and chaired the commission that drafted the Universal Declaration of Human Rights. She resigned from the UN delegation in 1952 but continued to give lectures around the world. She died in 1962.

was "the death of one era and the birth of another." The desire for reform in American government and politics was not new, and the president himself had come of political age during the Progressive movement of the early years of the 20th century.

What Roosevelt now proposed, however, while it was certainly in the spirit of the Progressive movement, was different in tone. It had less moral fervor to it and a healthy dose of pragmatism. But Roosevelt served warning right from the beginning that he had his sights on the commanding heights of the economy, when he referred scathingly to "economic royalists."

When Roosevelt took office, the economy was in a deplorable state, and the despairing mood simply reflected the reality. Unemployment figures had soared, and discontent had reached dangerous proportions. No president before had taken office when the economy was in such dire health.

In the past government reform had been directed at the needs of the entrepreneurial classes or those about to enter that class, including farmers, small businessmen, and professionals. The object of reform had been to make it easier for new men to get to the top and to curb abuses by monopolies and other entrenched interests. The free-enterprise or capitalist economic system was never in question, only the effectiveness and fairness of the way it operated.

A Pragmatic President

While Roosevelt himself was a product of that system, he seemed not to be much influenced by

economic theory of any kind. His basic instinct was for innovation and improvisation, which perfectly fitted a situation where the basic problem was near-paralysis in economic life. "It is common sense," he explained, "to take a method and try it. If it fails, admit it frankly and try another. But above all, try something." Trying something was to be the hallmark of FDR's New Deal.

The social and economic effect of the Depression had prepared public opinion for the new approach. It was now widely accepted that in order to achieve recovery, the federal government had to take responsibility for the conditions of the labor market. In particular the government could not ignore the plight of the unemployed. The labor movement had to be given recognition in order to implement codes of fair practice. Management and labor would have to pull together to get industry out of the slump.

Since the New Deal took shape at the same time as Nazi Germany was getting into its stride, some of his political enemies thought they

saw a parallel between Roosevelt's rapid, bold steps and the furious energy with which Adolf Hitler was imposing his will on Germany. Both leaders took over a nation in need of decisive action to extricate it from a crisis. The parallel ended there, however, since FDR's

•

"It is common sense to take a method and try it. If it fails… try another."

•

political pragmatism was harnessed to a vision of a just and humane society, while Hitler's vision was the polar opposite of everything FDR stood for.

Many liberals expected Roosevelt to deal harshly with the powerful economic interests that had failed the nation: the big corporations and monopolies. But he made little effort to interfere with

President Roosevelt's private study at the White House, with naval prints prominently displayed as always throughout his life.

FDR and members of his administration enjoy lunch at Camp Fechner, a Civilian Conservation Corps (CCC) camp at Big Meadows, Virginia, in 1933.

either. He showed himself happy to work with big business whenever, that is, big business would work with him. The need, as he saw it, was to get business back on its feet so that it could provide more jobs. Even critics of business interests could see sense in this approach.

Master of Communication

Roosevelt's efforts were characterized by his ability to deal with economic crisis and human need without tripping over accepted ideas and traditional inhibitions. His commitment to "bold, persistent experimentation" meant that the New Deal was not really a political philosophy but simply the practical application of ideas that seemed to make sense as the situation developed. It was not difficult to understand the direction of Roosevelt's policies, even if they changed tack from time to time, since the president himself seemed only too willing to explain his reasoning to his vast radio audience and in frequent press conferences. As the veteran humorist and actor Will Rogers (1879–1935) once dryly remarked, "Everybody understands him, even the bankers."

SEE ALSO

◆ Volume 2, Chapter 1, The Election of 1932

◆ Volume 2, Chapter 2, The First Hundred Days

◆ Volume 4, Chapter 1, Left vs. Right

◆ Volume 5, Chapter 1, Government, Industry, and Economic Policy

◆ Volume 5, Chapter 2, Equality for Some

◆ Volume 6, Chapter 6, The Legacy of the Depression

WHERE DID THE DEPRESSION BITE?

The Depression did not affect all Americans equally. It struck particularly at the middle classes, the poor, and vulnerable minorities: Many of the wealthiest citizens were largely insulated from its effects. Geographically, too, some regions suffered far worse than others.

When the stock market crashed in October 1929, it is estimated that around 36,000 of America's most affluent families enjoyed an income equal to that of the 10 million poorest families at the bottom of the economic scale. Many of the rich made huge losses in the crash, but their remaining wealth was enough to insulate them from the worst effects of the Depression. They still vacationed in Florida, bought fashions from Paris, and enjoyed traveling around the continent by airplane.

By contrast, the nation's poorer classes found themselves caught by the reversal in the economy. In the heady period of "Coolidge prosperity" in the second half of the 1920s many Americans saw their living standards rise (see Volume 1, Chapter 5, "The Fantasy World"). For some, however, the automobiles, re-

frigerators, radios, and fashions consumed a large proportion of their yearly income. Workers bought on credit and put in 12-hour days to keep up with the installment payments.

The loss of confidence after the crash encouraged the wealthy to stop investing in the stock market. As job losses followed (see Volume 3, Chapter 1, "Tough in the City"), the middle classes found

A destitute miner outside an abandoned zinc mine in Arkansas, 1935. Mining communities were among the worse hit by the economic downturn.

A family waits to hitch a lift outside Macon, Georgia, where they came to seek work. The father mended sewing machines, mowers, and other goods. Such services were in demand, but Macon imposed a $25 license for such work, and the family headed home to Alabama.

1. PEOPLE ON THE MOVE

One of the most significant consequences of the Depression was mass migration. At any time there were as many as five million Americans searching for work and themselves unable to pay their debts; they stopped buying new goods on credit. The vast armies of the poor—the farmers, African Americans, and recent immigrants, many of whom had long been excluded from the nation's prosperity—found themselves even worse off than before as wages tumbled.

ADAPTING TO CIRCUMSTANCE

The emotionally vulnerable were among those hit hardest. Some people found it impossible to accept unemployment and the loss of pride that it brought. The incidence of suicide and mental illness skyrocketed. Young graduates and businessmen would leave for work each day dressed in a suit to go door-to-door selling anything from ties to vacuum cleaners or to sell pencils or apples on street corners (see Volume 5, Chapter 3, "Society in the 1930s"). Waiting in breadlines or outside the employment office, lines of jobless people stuffed newspapers under their shirts to protect them from the cold and used pasteboard as inner soles in their shoes to protect their feet during long hours of pounding the pavements in search of work.

Poverty spread across much of the continent from late 1929 to 1933. The national income fell from $87 billion in 1930 to $40 billion in 1933; more than 18 million Americans depended on relief. It struck the agricultural heartlands of the Southern plantations, the Midwestern corn farms, and the grasslands of the Plains. It brought near-starvation to communities in the mountain country of Pennsylvania, West Virginia, and Kentucky. And it filled the parks of the nation's cities with thousands of dispossessed and homeless people living in cardboard and tar-paper shacks they wryly dubbed "Hoovervilles" for the president under whom they came into existence.

Shrinking Industries

As workers lost their jobs, businesses were unable to sell goods and services to them. Inevitably, production slowed. As the downward spiral began, more jobs were lost, and people began to default on their loans. As sales ebbed, industries laid off workers to cut costs. The new unemployed were in turn unable to buy goods from other industries, and further jobs were lost. The first industries to fall apart were the automobile and radio industries, which had been the object of both heavy investment and the credit-buying frenzy of the years leading up to the crash. Without cars, people did not need tires or fuel. Within the first four years of the Depression one-quarter of the total global wealth was destroyed, and production reduced by one half.

A hobo "jungle" near the riverfront at St. Louis, Missouri, in 1936. In many cases hobos fled bleak situations at home only to find themselves worse off in the poorest parts of towns and cities.

Peggy DeHart ran away from home at 15 after her father struck her for cursing at a cow on the family farm. "There was this girl called Irene Willis and she wanted to go to Issaquah to see her parents," DeHart recalls. "She was going to hitchhike and she asked me to come along. And I thought that was a great idea." DeHart sent letters to her family describing the tight situations she and Irene encountered: "The police picked up Reen and I last night and put us in a cell. We sure made use of the cots. I hope they run us loose so that we can go again. This is the third time they've picked us up."

Jim Mitchell left his Wisconsin home at the age of 16. Rene Champion was the same age when he left his home in Pennsylvania, as were John Fawcett from West Virginia and Bob "Guitar Whitey" Symmonds from Washington, D.C.,

fleeing despair. Travelers often crowded the roofs of freight trains and the doorways of boxcars. Some U.S. industries, particularly agriculture, had a tradition of migrant workers who moved from place to place for seasonal work. These transients were different, however. Most were seeking permanent resettlement after losing their jobs and their homes, and set out to find somewhere else. Many headed for states like Florida and California, with their warm climates and seasonal agriculture.

Most states established a Transient Bureau to give emergency care to nonresidents: In some instances they were wholly supported by federal funds, but the majority were run using a combination of federal and state funds. The program met with much opposition and criticism from those who feared that it aggravated an already troublesome problem by encouraging men and women who were unwilling, rather than unable, to work.

HOBOS

At the height of the Depression more than 250,000 teenagers were living as hobos. They left poverty and family problems behind and set off in search of what often seemed, at first, a great adventure. Virtually all of them began riding the railroads.

African American Transients

A large percentage of transients were African Americans, fleeing the appalling economic conditions they faced in the South. The relief they received was often less than that given to their white counterparts and varied greatly from city to city and state to state. Some northern states did, however, dispense relief equally among all needy citizens, regardless of creed or color. Statistics showed that the blacks who went to these northern states remained far longer than the transient whites. Illinois, in particular, became a stopping place for transients traveling from one part of the country to another, since it lay on a natural crossroads about midway between North, South, East, and West. The state housed white and black transients in segregated buildings, but relief provision was equal in all other ways. Again, black transients tended to stay in the shelters longer than the whites.

Tales from the Rails

Leslie E. Paul's vivid memories of leaving home in the summer of 1933 begin on the back porch of his house in Duluth. He was 18 years old, newly graduated from highschool, the son and stepson of railroad workers.

"I was a burden to Mother and Gus, my stepfather. I said nothing to Mother then, only that I was going down to Scott's to get a flat fifty box of cigarettes. Ordinarily I was reluctant to add to the delinquent account; today I found abundant courage. Besides the tin of cigarettes, I asked for two sacks of Golden Grain. 'Charge it,' I said. Scott looked taken aback but said nothing.

"I returned home and told Mother I was leaving. She didn't fight it, but she was sad. All she had was a black satin bag, the size of a pillow case. I jammed my new sleeping bag inside it, three or four pairs of socks, shorts, an old sweater, the cigarettes and sacks of Golden Grain. Mother made two sandwiches. She went to her purse and gave me all the money she had: 72 cents.

"I gave Mother a big kiss and a long, tight hug. She said nothing, but the tears streamed down her face. I turned and left, the black satin bag over my shoulder. Had I been brave enough, I would've been coward enough to go back. I stopped at the roundhouse and found Gus working on one of the engines. I owed him a lot. I had a roof over my head and there was always something to eat. I shook his hand and said good-bye.

"The freight yard was a terminal for trains going to Canada. My best bet was to go to Carleton, 19 miles away. The easiest way to get there was to walk. I crossed the tracks, climbed the fence and started up the hill to the highway. I turned around at the top. The tears came then, and one sob. The second one I swallowed. Every boy becomes a man, some younger, some older. I was eighteen and one week. Was I leaving little for nothing?"

who picked fruit in California to survive. In Louisiana Clarence Lee's father told him that there simply was not enough food to feed the family; the boy left home the next day to support himself. Lee was unable to hold back tears when he recalled the profound loneliness of his life at that time. "Some of it hurts now. I don't think I was twenty miles down the road riding in the blind of the car, and it was cold and miserable."

Jim Mitchell has similar memories: "Hell, I knew right then I had made a mistake. But you know, you're young and foolish and you don't say you made a mistake." Another traveler recalls receiving a cake sent by his mother for his 18th birthday and eating it alone on a hillside, in tears.

The young hobos traveled all over America, avoiding railroad police by jumping on and off moving freight trains—which was both illegal and highly dangerous. Many lost limbs, were killed, or arrested. It was a rough life of harsh lessons and extreme

Lower Douglas Street, Omaha, one of the hobo centers of the West. Hobos traveled from one center to the next, hoping to find work.

Loading coal in Jenkins, Kentucky, in October 1935. Shrinking demand for coal, coupled with fierce competition, forced many mines to close during the 1930s.

this was Belle Vernon, on the border of Fayette and Westmoreland counties in Pennsylvania state. Its entire population of 1,000 depended on a local industry called American Window Glass Company, the railroad, and a few small businesses. When the glass company shut down in the early years of the Depression, the whole town went on relief. A similar pattern was repeated throughout the United States.

Miners in the Appalachians

In the scattered mountain communities of western Pennsylvania, West Virginia, and Kentucky soft-coal miners suffered not only from the effects of the Depression, but also from competition from newer fuel resources, such as diesel oil, gas, and electricity. By contrast, recently discovered oilfields in southern California, Oklahoma, and west Texas gave those areas a new lease on life.

hardship and danger: The nights were cold, railroad guards were often brutal, and there were endless days of walking or hitch-hiking without food.

In 1933 Warner Brothers made a movie called *Wild Boys of the Road* in an attempt to scare some young people away from life on the railroads. In the film a boy falls on the tracks, and his leg is crushed by an oncoming train.

The teenage hobos continued to look for adventure, however. Most tried to earn money to send home to their families; but even when they did work, they received only a fraction of what an adult earned. Some went to New York in search of work, joined the bread-lines, and slept rough: others went west with a romantic dream of becoming cowboys.

2. RURAL AREAS

Economic conditions had been hard for people in America's rural areas for some time before the Depression hit. Farmers suffered especially, since many had gone

into debt to buy machinery and land during the boom years of World War I and now could not make their payments: Any profits they might make were wiped out by low crop prices (see Volume 3, Chapter 2, "Shadow over the Countryside"). As time went on, they became more desperate and increasingly militant.

THE NORTHEAST

In the northeastern states it was the small industrial communities, many of which depended on a single industry or factory, that fared the worst. One example of

A general provisions store with gasoline pumps in rural Pennsylvania around 1930. The western part of the state was devastated by the Great Depression.

An abandoned farm in Wisconsin. Many farmers left their farmsteads during the Depression and went to the towns and cities to find work or to go on the relief rolls.

Facing shrinking demand, oversupply, and bitter competition, operators in the coal mines cut prices and wages. The price of coal fell from as much as $4 a ton in the 1920s to $1.31 a ton in 1932. Miners who had earned $7 a day were now climbing into narrow coal seams for a daily wage of $1. United Mine Workers president John L. Lewis (1880–1969)

Unscrupulous Employer

In the small mining community of Elderville in Washington County, a mine was run by J. C. Cook on lease from a coal company in Pittsburgh, PA. When Cook defaulted on his royalty, he did not pay his miners their wages, so they walked out. The men had already lost money with their boss; when he had needed money the previous year, they had been told that they would have to assist him in purchasing stock in the mine if they wished to keep their jobs. Nearly all of the 150 miners were forced to buy $100 worth of stock— every new man hired was also required to purchase stock. When Cook defaulted on their wages, the whole workforce walked out. Shortly afterward, the mine was closed, and all the miners went on relief.

declared that the miners' diet was worse than many people fed to their domestic animals. Their children were malnourished and inadequately dressed, and vulnerable to a range of diseases, including tuberculosis, asthma, typhoid, and pellagra.

In 1932 only two-fifths of Pennsylvania's working population were in full-time employment. Some 1.1 million people were completely unemployed, and many others were working reduced hours. By 1933 well over half of the mining families in the Appalachian Mountains were entirely dependent on relief.

Dairy Farmers in Wisconsin

In early 1933 dairy farmers in Wisconsin stopped producing milk in a strike against the ever-increasing cost of production and the falling price. The unrest provoked a series of strikes that

lasted almost a year. As months went on and no response to their problems came from Washington, the dairy farmers became increasingly confrontational. At one point 5,000 strikers marched on the state capital in Madison. As the strike spread throughout the state, violence occasionally broke out, and farmers were injured. In Racine a guardsman shot a striker, and in Walworth County guards-

A scantily dressed sharecropper's child suffering from rickets and malnutrition plays on the Wilson cotton plantation, Mississippi County, Arkansas.

Mining in Fayette County

This letter describes the plight of the mining communities, whose diminishing livelihood was forcing the miners and their families to go on relief, with no prospects of the situation improving.

"It will be seen that life in Fayette County depends almost solely upon coal mining. There is some agriculture but the condition of this has been noted. As I said in my last letter, less than 50 of our more than 150 coal and coke plants are operating. It is admitted that a large proportion of those shut down never will reopen; many of those now operating have only a few years' coal ahead of them. Coal is 'going back' on the County; what was once a rich empire is almost ready to be dumped by its rulers; it has been bled white both above and below ground. Populations have been left stranded, not only without work, but without prospects of ever being re-employed in coal mining. What are they to do? Are they to remain indefinitely on direct relief? Will they have to move into other communities for possible absorption into other industries? Are they to be placed on homestead projects? What is going to happen to them? Every thoughtful person in Fayette is asking this question. All discussion concerning relief ends at this point. When I ask people for their impressions of the effect of relief they all take the short view. Perhaps the truth is that, so far as present relief is concerned, no other view can be taken—perhaps, so far as long range results are concerned, relief is having very little effect at all. It is helping the children. Malnutrition, which always has been the bane of child life on these depressing patches where for 40 years bare existence has been so pitiably sustained, is being reduced for the children are getting more milk from relief than they ever did from the best pay envelopes. That is something, but it is not enough, for the future of these youngsters under the present circumstances is hardly brighter than that of the parents.

"I do not know what the answer is. I have found no one who does. But, as [I] left Pennsylvania, one great need seemed to stand out clearly—the need for an intensive study of all these people—a careful survey by trained people of all these mining town populations, of the hill folk and of the areas harboring those stranded workers who have nothing in the present and even less in the future to contemplate. Possibly such a study would suggest a way out. I do not know; again I have found no one who does. There is nothing very hopeful or constructive in the mass of public opinion contacted in Western Pennsylvania."

Henry W. Francis

Striking miners draw rations in West Virginia. Wage cuts sparked many strikes, but many miners had to work for a fraction of their former pay.

men charged the pickets. By the end of the third strike eight cheese factories had been bombed and several creameries burned. In the end the Wisconsin farmers received no concessions to show for their months of strikes.

THE SOUTH

Many of the problems facing rural communities had roots that were far older than the Depression itself. During World War I the federal government had subsidized farms and paid high prices for wheat and other grain. Farmers were encouraged to buy land and modernize their equipment to feed the war effort. In the early 1920s the price for wheat had fallen dramatically, sending farmers into debt; now farm and food prices fell rapidly again. The farmers received little aid from the government. When banks began to foreclose on mortgages, many farmers lost everything.

Many of America's farmers and farm laborers had long lived from hand to mouth. Crops had been grown on soil that was not appropriate, or that had been overused until it was exhausted. In the rural South the situation was exacerbated by other characteristics of the region's agriculture. Farmers and their families generally lived on farms that were far too small to support them. They depended on single crops like cotton, tobacco, corn, or wheat that left them highly vulnerable to price fluctuations.

Cotton farming, in particular, relied on credit: Months before the crop was ready for harvest the tenant owed the landlord his rent, the landlord owed a merchant, the merchant owed a banker, and he in turn owed a larger financial organization. When banks began to close their doors and call in their loans, southern farmers were among the first to feel the pinch.

Sharecroppers and Tenant Farmers

The situation in the South was also worse because of its system of sharecroppers and tenant farmers. New Deal measures to reduce crop production by paying landowners to leave some of their fields uncultivated actually forced

Bewildered sharecropper families line a road near the Arkansas plantation from which they have just been evicted in January 1936. Their crime was joining the Southern Tenant Farmers' Union, an organization that protected tenants' rights. The families moved in to a tent colony.

many southern tenants and sharecroppers to leave the land they had farmed (see Volume 3, Chapter 6, "Continuing Plight of the Farmer").

The institution of tenancy had existed in the South since the Civil War; many of the tenant farmers were black. They farmed the land in return for giving their landlord a share of the crop and paying him for seed, equipment, and sometimes food. In many ways tenancy amounted to a system of agricultural servitude. The farming economy relied almost entirely on cotton, a crop that exhausted the land and provided no form of food for the people who grew it.

Tenant farming had created a layer of desperately poor whites and blacks who struggled to eat

Soil erosion in Alabama, 1935, caused by extreme weather conditions and farming methods that harmed the land.

and stay alive. The houses where they lived lacked sewers, piped water, and electricity, and were well below the level of similar housing in other parts of the country. Their children were often too poorly dressed to be able to attend school, and the overalls they wore to work were all they had for both summer and winter. They survived on a diet of grits, greens, and gravy. When the Depression hit, they were among America's most vulnerable citizens (see Volume 5, Chapter 2, "Equality for Some").

Migration to the Cities

When Southern farmers migrated to the cities, they found it equally difficult to make a living, having no suitable skills. With so many skilled and educated workers unemployed and

on the streets, most urban businesses had no need for this unskilled and uneducated labor from the South.

Industries in the South

Some members of the southern rural working community were accustomed to combine agriculture with industrial labor. During the harvest season they worked the fields; they rounded out their incomes by working the remainder of the year in the small marginal industries that had established themselves in the South in order to take advantage of the cheap labor supply. However, most of these small industries closed in the early years of the

Stripped of cover, this hillside in east Tennessee, pictured in 1936, is badly gullied by water runoff that washes away the valuable topsoil.

Depression because they could not compete with the northern factories once labor had become equally cheap throughout the United States. The workers who had been employed in these factories were among the many who migrated to the northern industrial centers to find work.

The Tennessee Valley

The Tennessee Valley was poor even by Depression standards. The Tennessee River ran through seven states, which were among the most disadvantaged in the South. Like the plains of the Dust Bowl, the land had been overfarmed for generations (see Volume 3, Chapter 3, "The Dust Bowl"). Without the benefit of modern agricultural methods the soil had been left to erode and deplete. The area was also prone to flooding, which further depleted the land of this already poverty-stricken area. This meant that the crops yielded less, and farm incomes were poor. To add to the region's problems, it was poor in natural resources such as forests. In the 1920s President Calvin Coolidge had vetoed a plan to build dams in the valley to control flooding and generate cheap hydroelectricity. The Tennessee Valley would be singled out by Roosevelt's administration with the creation of the Tennessee Valley Authority (TVA) (see box, page 92).

THE MIDWEST

The Midwest was dominated by family farms. During the Depression many of these farms fell into debt; they were foreclosed on in great numbers. In North Dakota drought and grasshopper infestations added to the problem of severely depressed agricultural prices, forcing many families to go on relief. Federal journalist Lorena Hickok (see box, page 76) described South Dakota as the "Siberia" of the United States and added, "A more hopeless place I never saw."

The Dust Bowl

For years conservationists had been warning of an ecological catastrophe. Much of the agricultural land in the Midwest had been eroded and rendered infertile by poor farming practices as homesteaders tried to eke out a living for their families on small, overworked farms. In 1934 the National Recovery Board estimated that over 35 million acres of arable land had been destroyed and 125 million acres of topsoil almost entirely removed; they reckoned another 100 million acres were irretrievable. In an area

A family leaves the South Dakota drought area for the West in 1935. Thousands of people left states in the Midwest in the hope of finding work in the fertile valleys of California.

from Texas to the borders of Canada, as well as parts of the South, unexpected droughts, characterized by violent winds and dust storms, took place in 1931 and 1932. They turned the soil to dust that blew across the land in great black storms people called "rollers."

These conditions endured throughout the 1930s but were particularly bad from 1935 to 1938, when crops were destroyed and machinery ruined. The situation was made worse by excessive plowing and overgrazing, and by the planting of wheat

instead of the native grasses that held the soil in place. The area also suffered intense fluctuations of temperature and low rainfall, which made the soil vulnerable to erosion. In 1934 record-breaking high temperatures killed hundreds of people in Colorado, Texas, Oklahoma, and Kansas.

By 1935 droughts had left 80 percent of the region in some stage of erosion. On the Great Plains dust storms stripped the topsoil. Intense heat killed livestock, and plagues of grasshoppers devoured crops and practically anything else in their path. Despite these con-

Migrant workers cut lettuce in Salinas, California, in June 1935. California's fertile valleys attracted migrants from the Dust Bowl and beyond, but work in the so-called "factories-in-the-fields" was hard and badly paid.

ditions, farm incomes actually increased by 50 percent between 1932 and 1935. This, however, was mainly due to money from federal programs.

Migrant Workers

Nearly 800,000 people, often refered to as "Okies" or "Arkies," left Arkansas, Texas, Missouri, and Oklahoma to seek migrant farm work, mainly in California (see Volume 3, Chapter 4, "California in the 1930s"). These migrants were vividly portrayed in John Steinbeck's novel *The Grapes of Wrath*. They had little or no food, and the roadside camps where they usually lived were squalid. California was not the land of dreams they had expected. The migrants included not only farmers, but also professionals, retailers, and others whose livelihoods were connected in some way to farm communities. They found themselves having to compete with traditional migrant workers for seasonal jobs picking crops at very low wages.

Many of the major agricultural states had long depended on migrant labor to cope with the peak loads at harvest time. In the sugar-beet fields of Colorado, Nebraska, Wyoming, and southern Montana growers had relied for years on outside migrant laborers to do the back-breaking harvest at below subsistence pay.

Each region had its own crops, depending on its climate and soil conditions. The typical migrant worker would start cotton picking in southern Texas in June and work his way to the Great Plains, laboring to nearly Christmas. Then he would move to the valleys and start cutting spinach and gathering vegetables in the areas where they were grown. Many migrant workers lived out the rest of the year in the missions and flophouses of cities like Chicago, St. Paul, and Minneapolis, again at subsistence level.

The migrant worker's life had always been precarious at best. He had to take his chances with slack periods and crop failures. When seasons were abundant, so was the work. In some areas of the country, when there was a shortage of

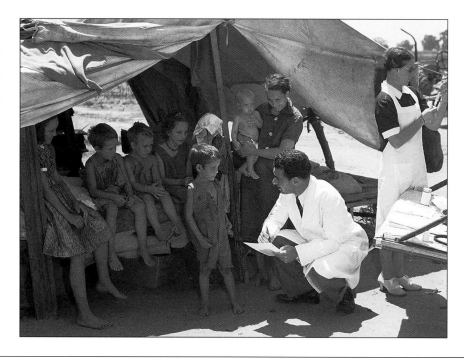

A doctor talks to migrant children in a California camp in 1939 as a nurse prepares vaccinations against smallpox and typhoid fever. Crowded and unsanitary camps made such diseases a real threat.

"Well, the Red Cross jest about saved our lives," said this Arkansas farmer, one of the victims of the drought of 1930–1931.

hands, children were sometimes forced to work in the fields.

The housing conditions were appalling, with workers usually compelled to live in one-room shacks devoid of sanitation. The wages were marginal and sub-marginal, and farmers would only pay cash after their crops had been marketed. They then haggled with their workforce over how much they had actually earned. It was also during the Depression that agricultural machinery became more common, reducing the demand for migrant laborers.

As New Deal relief programs kicked into action, many of these workers refused to harvest the fields because they received more on relief. This was particularly true among the traditional migrant workers: the former tramp workers who had passed their winters in the inner cities. In 1935 it was calculated that more than a million families who had been dependent on agriculture were now receiving public assistance. Once they had done this, they were often afraid to work in case they would not be able to get back into the relief programs. Such a situation existed in all agricultural areas where seasonal labor was required.

3. URBAN CENTERS
The unemployed from the countryside, towns, and smaller cities flocked to larger cities in search of work. However, they found life in the big cities could be even tougher: They could not raise their own food there (see Volume 3, Chapter 1, "Tough in the City"). Every night in cities such as New York, Detroit, and

Seattle, hungry people scavenged for scraps of food on garbage dumps and in garbage cans.

It was once again the unskilled and poorest laborers who fared the worst. Early on in the Depression President Hoover had attempted to provide some indirect relief through public works projects (see Volume 1, Chapter 7: "Hoover: The Search for a Solution"). They proved ineffective because they could only employ a limited number of people with certain skills: Huge numbers of white-collar and unskilled workers were excluded. White-collar workers sometimes had the biggest psychological problems facing up to unemployment because they could not do most regular relief work but detested having to rely on home relief.

NEW YORK
New York was one of the cities where the unemployed flocked in search of work, only to end up with the other million unemployed in one of the city's

breadlines. In 1931 Roosevelt, who at the start of the Depression was governor of New York State, introduced some of the country's most radical legislation to fight the effects of unemployment. By 1932, not long before his election as president, approximately 10 percent of the state's families were receiving relief of about $23 per month. As small an amount as this was, it kept families from starving. By comparison, relief payments in Detroit were 5 cents a day per person, or about $1.50 a month, and $3.00 a month in Illinois.

DETROIT
In 1929 the General Motors plant in America's automobile capital, Detroit, laid off 100,000 workers out of a total 260,000. By 1932 there were 223,000 unemployed wandering the streets of the city. Men waited all night outside Detroit employment offices in the hope of being the first in line when the offices opened in the morning. In 1935 the industrial city still had a quarter of a million people on relief, and the unemployed population ranged between 50,000 and 75,000 people. This was due, in part, to large groups of workers who came to the city in the early years of the Depression in search of work.

Some unscrupulous automotive companies had actually sent labor agents to recruit hillbillies from Kentucky, Tennessee, Louisiana, and Alabama. These impoverished rural whites had little or no contact with modern industry and labor unions. They would accept lower wages, and there was little risk of them unionizing. Management was in control, and the working population was desperate. If workers walked off the job and picketed a

Lorena Hickok (1893–1968)

Lorena Hickok, known as "Hick," was one of the most influential reporters in the early years of the Depression. She was a physically large presence and had an equally large personality, an unconventional streak, and a penchant for drinking and smoking.

Hickok was born in 1893 in East Troy, Wisconsin and grew up on the northern plains. She embarked on a journalistic career as a feature writer in Milwaukee and Minneapolis before moving to New York, where she accepted a job in 1928 as a hard-news reporter with Associated Press—an unusual role for a woman at that time. Four years later she covered the Lindbergh baby kidnapping (see Volume 3, Chapter 5, "Crime in the Depression"). That same year—1932—Hickok was assigned the job of covering Eleanor Roosevelt during the presidential campaign. She became very close to the First Lady and questions about their friendship led to Hickok's resignation from Associated Press in June 1933.

The following month the director of the Federal Emergency Relief Administration, Harry Hopkins, assigned Hickok the task of traveling around the country and writing field reports on what she observed in the different states. His instructions to her were clear: "I don't want statistics from you. I don't want the social-worker angle. I just want your own reaction, as an ordinary citizen."

Hickok set off on her mission to interview as wide a cross-section of the American population as she could find, from plantation owners to miners, housewives and sharecroppers, local businessmen and unemployed destitutes. She stayed in simple hotels in the Appalachian coal-mining districts of West Virginia and Pennsylvania, the Dust Bowl states of Colorado and Kansas, the cotton country of Alabama and Texas, and the depressed Tennessee Valley, tapping out her interviews on a rickety typewriter. Soon her reports were winging their way to Hopkins in Washington. He read them with great interest and concern, remarking that they would be "the best history of the Depression in future years."

As Hickok continued her travels through the different states, she began to realize that the scenes

Lorena Hickok and Eleanor Roosevelt on a fact-finding visit to Puerto Rico in 1934. The two women shared a commitment to the relief of poverty.

of poverty and destitution she encountered were not purely of the Depression's making, but had existed for a long time before the financial crash. Of the miners in West Virginia, for example, she observed that "Some of them have been starving for eight years." She was even more shocked by scenes she saw in the South of "half-starved Whites and Blacks struggling in competition for less to eat than my dog gets at home." Further, she was horrified by the attitudes of relief officials in North Dakota who thought "there is something wrong with a man who cannot make a living." In Hickok's opinion such people, steeped in the ways of a longtime unequal society, had neither the insight nor the will to change the situation.

Poor health forced Hickok to retire from political life in 1945. She moved into a cottage in Hyde Park near the Roosevelt estate and wrote numerous books on the lives of Eleanor and Franklin Roosevelt. She died in 1968 at the age of 75, virtually forgotten. Nobody claimed her cremated ashes, and they were finally buried alongside other unclaimed ashes at Rhinebeck Cemetery.

The interior of a typical Kentucky mountaineer home, 1930–1931. A 70-year-old grandfather cooks his ration of Red Cross bacon over a fire for himself and his grandson.

plant, management could bring in new workers to break the strike. Many workers were obliged to accept any working conditions put before them as long as they could work (see Volume 4, Chapter 6, "The Unionization of Labor"). There was always a long line of unemployed waiting for their job.

CHICAGO

Chicago's steel industry was hit badly by the Depression. As a result, by the end of 1931 the number of unemployed in the city had reached 624,000. Black workers, who made up 4 percent of the population, suffered more than others, accounting for 16 percent of the city's unemployed.

4. THE RELIEF PROBLEM

With the New Deal the federal government recognized the necessity for direct relief on a massive scale (see Volume 4, Chapter 5, "Relief"). It was to take the form of home relief, direct payments to the indigent (much the way welfare works today), and work relief to provide jobs for the unemployed.

With so many skilled laborers and so little work, the least skilled, along with ethnic and immigrant minorities, were the first to lose their jobs. This situation remained throughout the early years of the Depression. A New York City employment agency had 5,000 applications for 300 jobs. There were sweatshops in Brooklyn where young teenagers worked 50-hour weeks for $2.78 and women received even less. In the textile mills of New England teenage girls worked nonstop from before dawn until after dark. Unscrupulous employers pushed down wages until desperate employees would work nine hours and take home $1.00. These practices made it virtually impossible for honest employers to survive the competition; they went out of business, and the welfare lines grew ever longer. Municipal and state governments were faced with the perplexing problem of giving these starving masses relief so that they could eat without losing their morale and independence or breaking their spirits.

PRIVATE CHARITIES

At the onset of the Depression charities provided much of the aid to the unemployed and needy. However, these private institutions quickly ran out of funds when contributors lost their livelihoods and fortunes. By 1932 only 6 percent of the money spent on the poor came from private sources, leaving some 20 million—and perhaps up to 30 million—Americans relying on the public sector for support.

STATE AND LOCAL GOVERNMENT AID

Local governments and charities saw their resources dry up. In fact, state and local governments had been running in the red since 1930. Most municipal income came from taxation on real estate, but landlords were not able to pay these taxes if the tenants who occupied their property were unable to pay the rents. Many landlords tried to collect their rent money or put whole families on the street. However, empty tenement blocks did not solve the problem—there was no one able to move in. Local governments became so short of funds that it became increasingly difficult to be put on the welfare and relief rolls. In order to be considered, a family had to sell all its possessions, have all credit and insurance canceled, and provide

Life in the Cities

Richard Waskin talks about life during the Great Depression. His parents were born in Poland. He was born in East Chicago, Indiana. When he was three years old, he went back to Poland with his parents. They returned to the United States the following year and came to the Detroit area, where he spent most of his life.

"Mostly I remember if it hadn't been for my mother, who was an excellent seamstress, and she seemed to find jobs here and there with the department stores, I don't know how we would have made it, because my father was a common laborer, a factory worker, and there just wasn't any jobs at that time.

"Sometimes during the winter...when the snow fell in Detroit they called for people that they wanted to shovel the snow, and of course everybody didn't get hired—you just had to go out there and the foreman or whoever would be throwing the shovel and if you happened to catch it you're hired. And so my father would go out there and on occasion he would be hired and earn a couple of dollars or so for the day's work there....

"Well, there's one thing that happened with me and perhaps I was fortunate that Detroit had...a welfare system.... One of the things was that I came down with a mastoid which was a very serious thing at that time. It's very rare now because of antibiotics. But my whole side of my head was swollen and they called what they called 'a city physician.' And at that time doctors made house calls. So he came out and took one look at my head and he called the ambulance immediately and they took me to Children's Hospital 'cause I was only 11 years old. And they operated on me that night and I must assume that that saved my life at that time.

"But another thing as a child that I remember was that you stood in the welfare line somewhere on Michigan Avenue...and they were passing out sweaters for children and we were fortunate enough to get me a grey sweater, and I can remember how proud I was of having that sweater and how warm I felt with that thing on. Shoes, of course, were a problem and many times I remember I wore out the soles down to the pavement, so to speak, and you had to put cardboard in there. But then my father he got hold of some shoe forms—metal ones—and he would buy leather. He would cut out the sole—with nails and a hammer on these shoe forms—he would put new leather on my shoes and probably on my brothers' also...."

People stand in line for handouts of food in New York City. This was an all-too-familiar sight in America's cities during the Depression years.

proof that all known relations were also without financial means. In some cities no assistance was given to anyone single or without children. In the majority of cities only 25 percent of families qualifying for assistance actually received any.

Bankruptcy also affected public employees such as teachers, who found themselves either jobless or working without pay. By 1932, 300,000 children were out of school due to a lack of local funds to keep the schools open. In Dayton, Ohio, schools were only open three days a week. In New York City, during the same year, the welfare council reported 139 deaths caused by starvation and malnutrition; most of the victims were children.

There were scenes of great kindness and great intolerance. In Lewiston, Maine, in 1932 welfare recipients were barred from voting,

People gardening in Lancaster County, Pennsylvania, 1932. The Red Cross supplied 2,500 pounds of seed for city and county gardens.

and in some communities taxpayer associations tried to prevent welfare children from attending school and families receiving public assistance from attending church. On the other side police officers in New York City had been distributing food since 1930. Public servants in that same city donated 1 percent of their salaries for the same purpose. This solidarity with the poor and suffering came from the lower ranks of public service—welfare workers, the police, and teachers. They were often indistinguishable from the destitute since they relied on the same public coffers.

CHARITY FROM THE RICH

Millions of people around the country stayed alive living like animals, eating wild weeds and roots. In the cities families dived into garbage dumps for anything that they could find. The wealthy gave their refuse to charity to feed the starving. An Oklahoma gas-board executive organized a plan whereby civic clubs, restaurants, and hotel chefs would donate five-

gallon packs of refuse to the Salvation Army to be handed out to the needy.

The social tensions created by the Depression were clearly visible. During the worst years there were persistent protests by farmers, workers, war veterans, and people who were simply hungry. The distinctions between the poor and rich challenged the social peace. It became obvious after the first years of the New Deal that much of the population suffered the same inequalities that had always existed, and that the sporadic remedies of the early Roosevelt acts were not enough to lift the underprivileged out of their misery. Unemployment among the most needy persisted, although the majority were, by 1935, given financial relief of some sort.

SEE ALSO

◆ Volume 3, Chapter 1, Tough in the City

◆ Volume 3, Chapter 2, Shadow over the Countryside

◆ Volume 3, Chapter 3, The Dust Bowl

◆ Volume 3, Chapter 4, California in the 1930s

◆ Volume 3, Chapter 5, Crime in the Depression

◆ Volume 3, Chapter 6, Continuing Plight of the Farmer

◆ Volume 5, Chapter 2, Equality for Some

◆ Volume 5, Chapter 3, Society in the 1930s

PUTTING PEOPLE TO WORK

Of the many interrelated problems afflicting the nation in the spring of 1933 none was more pressing than the curse of unemployment, which had cast millions of Americans into hardship and penury. Much of the legislation rushed onto the statute books during the Hundred Days was aimed squarely at job creation, which would be a defining characteristic of the Roosevelt New Deal. Some of the job creation plans were very successful, others less so, but taken together they demonstrated a commitment to the principle that the opportunity to work was an important basic freedom.

As the 73rd Congress adjourned on June 16, 1933, it could credit itself with the greatest burst of legislative activity in the history of the republic. In step with the dynamic

Heavy construction work was a dominant theme in projects established by the Works Progress Administration. For example, some 600,000 miles of rural roads were repaired between 1935 and 1943.

leadership provided by President Roosevelt it had passed 15 major pieces of legislation in a little over three months and had fundamentally changed the political landscape. The Agricultural Adjustment Administration, the Civilian Conservation Corps, the Farm Credit Administration, the Federal Deposit Insurance Corporation, the Federal Emergency Relief Administration, the National Recovery Administration, the Public Works Administration, and the Tennessee Valley Authority—these and the other measures implemented during the Hundred Days constituted a massive extension of the federal government into the nation's economic and social life (see Chapter 2, "The First Hundred Days").

1. THE NEW DEAL TAKES SHAPE

The New Deal that Roosevelt had promised in his nomination speech the year before was in place—that is to say, the federal government was actively, almost frenziedly, engaged in the task of trying to lift the United States out of the Great Depression. Central to that task was getting people back to work. With the unemployment figure standing at 25 percent this was central to national recovery. All the attendant evils of the greatest economic setback in the nation's history—poverty, hunger, homelessness, despair—led back to the scourge of unemployment. The New Deal would be judged by its effectiveness in combating that scourge.

THE CIVILIAN CONSERVATION CORPS

Within three weeks of his inauguration Roosevelt had set in motion his first program for the unemployed in the form of the Civilian Conservation Corps (CCC), established with the purpose of bringing relief to young men between 18 and 25 years of age. The Corps was to be run in semimilitaristic fashion.

The CCC was Roosevelt's pet project, and partly thanks to the Army involvement it was an instant success. While it was headed by the civilian Robert Fechner, the vice-president of the American Federation of Labor, it was organized by General Douglas MacArthur (1880–1964). Other military notables made their reputations running CCC camps before going on to lead the Allied forces to victory a decade later during World War II. General George C. Marshall (1880–1969) ran 17 camps in the South, and Major Dwight D. Eisenhower (1890–1969), future president, ran the camps in Pennsylvania.

Two million young men took part in the program during the 10 years of its existence and participated in a variety of conservation projects: from planting

CCC youths in Idaho's Salmon National Forest, removing beaver from a ranch where they are devouring crops to a nearby river.

Upbeat poster spelling out the joys of the CCC. The link between paid work and the camaraderie of the camps was a draw for the young.

trees to combating soil erosion and maintaining national forests; eliminating stream pollution; creating fish, game, and bird sanctuaries; and conserving coal, petroleum, shale, gas, sodium, and helium deposits. The CCC was officially inaugurated on April 5, 1933, and the first camp was opened 12 days later.

The CCC was finally hope for the millions of teenagers and young adults who had drifted from city to city in search of a better existence. On June 8 more than 80,000 men were established in 400 forest camps, while 155,000 were in what were called conditioning camps for basic training.

They were subsequently transferred to the work camps at the rate of nearly 9,000 a day.

A Huge Catchment

Those sent to the conditioning camps in preparation for placement in the Corps camps were not only teenagers, since the program was quickly expanded to encompass members of the various needy groups of men in distress, including war veterans and disadvantaged ethnic minorities. More than 3,000 Native Americans were accepted for conditioning immediately, with a total quota of 14,400. Alaska had a quota of 325 and Puerto Rico 1,200 (see Volume 5, Chapter 2, "Equality for Some").

All this was put into effect within the first month of the CCC's operation. In these original corps 8,000 unemployed war veterans were assigned to erosion control work in Vermont. They came from New York, 2,575; Pennsylvania, 1,950; Massachusetts, 875; New Jersey, 825; Connecticut, 325; Rhode Island, 150; Maine, 150; New Hampshire, 100; and Vermont, 75.

From Coast to Coast

The army posts and stations that were set aside for conditioning the men were immediately filled to capacity. Men were sent across the United States from the East, where there were only a few forest work projects, to the heavily forested areas of the West Coast, although every attempt was made to send men to work on projects in their own states. On May 24, little more than a month after the CCC's initiation, the transportation of men from the East to the West began when the cadets of 32 companies were dispatched to Utah and Idaho from Fort

The President Explains the CCC

In his message to Congress calling for the establishment of the CCC Roosevelt eloquently expressed the rationale for it:

"The first of these measures which I have enumerated…can and should be immediately enacted. I propose to create a civilian conservation corps to be used in simple work not interfering with normal employment, and confining itself to forestry, the prevention of soil erosion, flood control, and similar projects. I call your attention to the fact that this type of work is of definite practical value, not only through the prevention of great present financial loss, but also as a means of creating future national wealth. This is brought home by the news we are receiving today of vast damage caused by floods on the Ohio and other rivers. Control and direction of such work can be carried on by existing machinery of the departments of Labor, Agriculture, War and Interior.

"I estimate that 250,000 men can be given temporary employment by early summer if you give me authority to proceed within the next two weeks.

"I ask no new funds at this time. The use of unobligated funds, now appropriated for public works, will be sufficient for several months.

"This enterprise is an established part of our national policy. It will conserve our precious natural resources. It will pay dividends to the present and future generations. It will make improvements in national and state domains which have been largely forgotten in the past few years of industrial development.

"More important, however, than the material gains will be the moral and spiritual value of such work. The overwhelming majority of unemployed Americans, who are now walking the streets and receiving private or public relief, would infinitely prefer to work. We can take a vast army of these unemployed out into healthful surroundings. We can eliminate to some extent at least the threat that enforced idleness brings to spiritual and moral stability. It is not a panacea for all the unemployment but it is an essential step in this emergency. I ask its adoption."

CCC boys quarrying rock in Missouri. Roosevelt stressed that the CCC served several purposes. The work was productive and in line with conservation goals, it provided employment for the young, and it did so in healthy outdoor environments.

Slum housing in Atlanta, Georgia, scheduled to be replaced by the Housing Division of the PWA in 1934 (see caption page 86).

Monroe, Virginia, and Fort Meade, Maryland. Each train carried 16 regular Army officers, 64 enlisted men, and 336 members of the CCC.

By the beginning of July 250,000 young people were settled in nearly 1,500 forest and park camps. The camps also provided jobs for approximately 16,000 civilians. They included construction foremen and supervisors, who were needed to oversee the work of the Civilian Conservation Corps.

Looking after Morale

In order to maintain morale and discipline in the camps, early in June President Roosevelt gave an executive order increasing the cash allowances to be paid for 13 percent of the men enrolled in the Corps and a new penalty system

for minor offenses committed by the enrolled personnel. The new regulations provided that not more than 5 percent of the authorized strength of any Civilian Conservation Corps company could be paid a cash allowance of $45 a month, while an additional 8 percent could be paid a cash allowance of $36 a month. The previous regulations provided for a flat cash allowance of $30 a month for each enrolled man. It was the job of the company commander and the camp superintendent to decide who would receive these higher cash allowance rates.

The penalty system was similar to those imposed in industry to maintain efficiency of production and create equality in opportunity and privileges. These included admonition, suspension of privileges, substitution of specified duties within the camp for a period of up to a week, or deduction of up to three days of cash allowance per month. The camps had welfare

and recreational programs, and each camp was supplied with athletic equipment, newspapers, and magazines.

Openings for African Americans

Six Civilian Conservation Corps camps were established in Milwaukee County, Wisconsin, to employ single, unemployed young men, aged 17 through 28. These camps, unlike those in northern Wisconsin, were open to African Americans as well as whites. The CCC crews laid jetties into Lake Michigan to control erosion at Sheridan Park, excavated rock and dirt, and built dams on the Milwaukee River to control flooding, landscaped miles of parkway, and developed large sections of Whitnall Park.

In the Southwest and in California CCC crews worked on projects for reforestation, forest fire hazard removal, improvements such as telephone lines, truck trails, footpaths, firebreaks, docks, fire lookout towers, ranger stations, and cabins. At the same time, 8,000 unemployed war veterans from nine eastern states were sent to Vermont on flood control work.

In some areas the men worked on water development projects and the improvement of camp grounds. Many were assigned to forest work, including cutting down some trees to allow preferred species the possibility of better growth as well as eradication of insect infestations.

A Successful Program

Within three years 1,150,000 men had passed through the Corps, to emerge for the most part healthier, more self-disciplined, and with much improved morale as they set about looking for employment.

Along with this the Civilian Conservation Corps had achieved protection and improvement of the nation's forests, arrested soil wastage, developed recreational areas, and made a contribution to wildlife conservation and flood control. It is small wonder that the Civilian Conservation Corps was the most universally applauded measure of the New Deal and perhaps the best example of Roosevelt's gift for capitalizing on the suddenly progressive mood of the American people as a whole.

THE PUBLIC WORKS ADMINISTRATION

Two of FDR's appointees became especially closely identified with tackling unemployment: Harry Hopkins (1890–1946) and Harold Ickes (1874–1952). Hopkins was at the center of most of the major relief agencies for the first five years of the administration. Ickes, as secretary of the interior, ran the vast Public Works Administration (PWA). As one of the first New Deal projects the PWA provided employment as well as helping change the face of America by building public works.

A Colossal Undertaking

By 1939, when it was discontinued, the PWA had completed over 34,000 construction projects—schools, city halls, hospitals, bridges, libraries, and the nation's first public housing—at a cost of more than $6 billion.

The Housing Division of the PWA constructed housing throughout the United States. At its creation the plan was to have 60 federal housing projects under

The CCC fostered a spirit of enthusiasm among the young who took up the challenge, and this was reflected by the public at large.

construction by December 1935. The provisions were for the purpose of cleaning up slums and erecting low-rent dwellings. The funds were advanced in the form of loans or outright grants. The money was also available to private companies in the form of loans.

The federal housing projects were part of the administration's battle against indecent housing conditions (see Volume 4, Chapter 5, "Welfare"). Twenty-eight of the projects were in black slum areas. They were to provide affordable income for about 23,000 low-income black families. Their cost represented 29 percent of the total federal funds for slum clearance developments. The projects were in seven cities: Atlanta, Cleveland, Detroit, Indianapolis, Montgomery, Chicago, and Nashville.

They were among the earliest federal housing projects initiated by the PWA.

THE CIVIL WORKS ADMINISTRATION

Work relief also came in the form of the Civil Works Administration, under Harry Hopkin's dynamic leadership. Although criticized as "make work," the jobs it funded ranged from ditch digging and highway repairs to teaching. Roosevelt created it in November 1933 because he realized that recovery was coming too slowly to provide a substantial enough increase in jobs by the time winter set in. And the PWA would not be in full swing before 1934. The CWA was a temporary measure to bridge that gap and was abandoned in the spring of 1934.

Roosevelt's Right-hand Man

Harry Hopkins was perhaps the single most influential of all the New Dealers. In May 1933 FDR brought a man to Washington who had nothing to do with the profession of politics: Harry Hopkins had, in fact, been working in New York City fighting the Depression as a social worker. He had worked closely with Governor Roosevelt in implementing the New York Temporary Relief Agency, a public relief exercise in response to the Depression that presaged the New Deal. On becoming president, Roosevelt gave Hopkins the principal responsibility for organizing public relief on a vast scale. Between 1933 and 1938, when ill health forced him to lay down such heavy administrative burdens, Hopkins was variously in charge of the Federal Emergency Relief Administration, Civil Works Administration, the Federal Surplus Relief Administration, and the Works Progress Administration.

To these tasks Hopkins brought an unmatched enthusiasm. No theoretician, he drove himself and his staff mercilessly in pursuit of his purely practical goals of getting relief to the people who needed it. He was responsible for allocating billions of dollars, and he was legendary for his incorruptibility. A famous cartoon of 1936 shows a smiling Hopkins putting up a plaque to his own memory at the WPA headquarters. It reads, "To the everlasting honor of Harry L. Hopkins...who spent $9 billions of his country's money and not a dollar stuck to his fingers." Hopkins went on during World War II to serve FDR as a trusted adviser and diplomat. He died in 1946.

The procedures of the CWA were in keeping with the strong preference that Roosevelt and his key officials had for unemployment programs based on work relief rather than welfare. In its short existence the CWA made a considerable impact, with four million unemployed working under its auspices by the end. It was bankrolled by $400 million of public funds. As one of the first of the New Deal projects it reflected what became known as the philosophy of the New Deal: "A CWA project must be one which directly or indirectly contributes to the construction of something; mere housekeeping is not included." This meant anything from building repair, such as painting, electrical wiring, paper hanging, and roof repairs, to furniture repair and the updating of sanitary equipment.

An architect's drawing of the ambitious WPA housing project designed to replace the black slum area shown on page 84.

UNIVERSITY HOUSING PROJECT FOR NEGROES · ATLANTA GEORGIA
WARDS·SAYWARD ARCHITECTS ·· ROBERT LOGAN·ASSOCIATE
O I FREEMAN ENGINEER
1934

When federal funds became available under the Civil Works Administration, with only three weeks of planning time Milwaukee city and county officials developed projects to employ 26,000 workers during the winter of 1933 to 1934 in landscaping, road grading, street repair, and painting.

One of the largest projects employed almost 2,000 men straightening out an S-curve in the Milwaukee River and constructing a lagoon and islands in Lincoln Park in order to reduce flooding on the north side of Milwaukee. County park projects included construction of a quarry at Currie Park, construction of two swimming pools, and extending electrical and telephone wiring to county parks and golf courses.

THE NATIONAL RECOVERY ADMINISTRATION

Most ambitious of all the New Deal enterprises was the National Recovery Administration (NRA), set up during the Hundred Days. The aim of the NRA was to fix wages and prices, shorten working hours, and regulate production. Its aim was to do this through organizing the national economy, industry by industry. The theory was that planning would prevent further economic instability and promote the growth needed to end the Depression. The NRA was established by the National Industry Recovery Act (NIRA), which also attempted to bring an end to cut-throat competition. This extremely ambitious and complex legislation was conceived to create a partnership between government and industry, something that had never been attempted in peacetime.

In addition, the NRA was to establish codes of practice to generate more jobs and thus

Installation of water mains in Minnesota in 1934, carried out by the CWA. Roosevelt insisted that all CWA projects involve construction.

stimulate purchasing power. Initially it was welcomed by and large across the board; but as recovery began, business resented the over-regulation and the loss of power to the labor force (see Volume 4, Chapter 4, "The Right-Wing Backlash"). In the first year nine million workers benefited from the NRA's wage codes, and one million employers joined the campaign. However, most of them

were small businesses, many in the textile industry; it took larger industry much longer to sign up, and the automobile and coal industries were among the last to fall under the NRA umbrella. The fiercely independent-minded Henry Ford never took part.

The Blue Eagle

The NRA's greatest contribution was probably in its creation of a temporary "wartime"-like unity. General Hugh Johnson (1882–1942), administrator of the NRA, designed the Blue Eagle as its symbol, and its slogan was "We do

CWA road construction in Minnesota. Over 250,000 miles of road were built or improved during the CWA's brief existence.

through unions of their choice, and prohibited employers from interfering in union activities. At the same time, it created the National Labor Relations Board to

•

"God have mercy on ... men who trifle with this bird."

•

supervise collective bargaining and ensure that workers could choose the organization representing them in dealing with employers.

These major advances brought working people together with a sense of common interests, and labor's power increased not only in industry but also in politics; the Democratic Party generally received more union support than the Republicans because it was seen as being more sympathetic to the union point of view.

our part." Johnson was fierce in his protection of the NRA. It was reported that, when questioned about the growing criticism of the NRA, he growled to the press, "God have mercy on the man or group of men who trifle with this bird." Firms that complied with the NRA's codes could display Blue Eagles on their documents or in their windows, and their employees wore the eagles on their uniforms. *Time* magazine displayed the eagle on its cover, and children in a San Francisco baseball park sat in a formation of a Blue Eagle to promote the agency.

In its first year the Blue Eagle campaign spread like a fever, and there was hardly a town or city that did not have a parade or rally to celebrate and promote the Blue Eagle. "Happy Days Are Here Again," Roosevelt's campaign song

from the 1932 election, was the theme song. Government agencies would only deal with Blue Eagle registered companies.

The NRA was effectively ruled unconstitutional by the Supreme Court in 1935 (see Volume 4, Chapter 2, "The Supreme Court"). The only part of its underlying legislation that survived the court became the core of the National Labor Relations Act, which organized labor has honored as its "bill of rights" since.

THE NATIONAL LABOR RELATIONS ACT

It was during this period that organized labor made its greatest strides (see Volume 4, Chapter 6, "The Unionization of Labor"). The NIRA guaranteed labor's right to collective bargaining (another facet of the act disliked and opposed by industry). In 1935 Congress passed the National Labor Relations Act. It defined unfair labor practices, gave workers the right to bargain

AGRICULTURAL ADJUSTMENT ADMINISTRATION

The Agricultural Adjustment Administration (AAA) was another key provision of the New Deal. It was created by the Agricultural Adjustment Act during the Hundred Days to provide immediate relief to farmers (see Volume 3, Chapter 2, "Shadow over the Countryside"). In the longer term the AAA was seen to rationalize the farming industry. The basic principle of the AAA was to raise crop prices by paying farmers subsidies to take their crops out of production. Between 1932 and 1935 farm incomes increased by more than 50 percent. The funding for the subsidies came from a tax that was levied on the

industries that processed the crops, such as flour mills.

By the time the AAA became law, it was well into the 1933 growing season, and the new legislation actually required that farmers destroy crops. Secretary of Agriculture Henry A. Wallace (1888–1965) called it a "shocking commentary on our civilization." However, with the help of the AAA and the Commodity Credit Corporation, a program that extended loans for crops kept in storage and off the market, farming output dropped, and prices began to go up.

Although the AAA chalked up many successes, it was abandoned in 1936, when the tax on the food-processing industry was ruled unconstitutional. Congress then passed a more effective farm relief act, which authorized payments to farmers who reduced plantings of soil-depleting crops—thereby achieving crop reduction through soil conservation (see Volume 3, Chapter 6, "Continuing Plight of

A vast CWA project involving 6,000 men engaged in road building in San Francisco in 1934. By the spring of that year more than four million unemployed men were at work on CWA projects nationwide.

Roosevelt's Riposte

When the Supreme Court struck down the NRA by a unamimous vote in May 1935, the president reacted in fury. He considered the NRA the centerpiece of his New Deal and was vehement in his denunciation of the ruling. In response he urged a wide range of new reforms, some much more radical than those of the New Deal to date. This second burst of legislation became known as the second New Deal.

the Farmer"). The Soil Conservation Act was replaced by the second AAA in 1938. By 1940 nearly six million farmers were receiving federal subsidies. The new act provided loans on surplus crops, insurance for wheat, and planned storage to ensure a stable food supply. Commodity prices rose, and economic stability for the farmer began to seem possible.

WORKS PROGRESS ADMINISTRATION
On May 6, 1935, FDR created the Works Progress Administration (WPA) by executive decree. He did so in the face of an unemployment figure that remained stubbornly around 20 percent, and he was concerned that long-term unemployment was bound to undermine the victims' "self-respect, their self-confidence and courage and determination."

The WPA was the principal relief agency during the second New Deal (see Chapter 6, "The Election of 1936"). Under the

A WPA class in automobile mechanics in Phoenix, Arizona, in 1936. Raising skills levels was an important feature of the WPA.

WPA buildings, roads, airports, and schools were constructed. Between 1935 and 1943, when the war effort made it redundant, it was a national work relief program of huge scope. The WPA spent $11 billion and employed three million people, mainly in construction, and changed the face of America. In a single year the WPA built or improved 140,000 miles of roads and streets. It constructed 1,500 athletic fields and playgrounds, 250 swimming pools, and 45 airports. It dug 4,000 miles of sewers for 500,000 new sanitary toilets. It built 4,500 public buildings, renovated 12,000 public buildings, repaired and catalogued 22 million books in public libraries, planted 5 million trees, and drained 500,000 acres.

A Vast Array of Projects

In New York City alone the WPA built the Lincoln Tunnel connecting New York and New Jersey under the Hudson River, and the Triborough Bridge linking Manhattan to Long Island. Major construction projects within New York State included the Loudonville Reservoir in Albany, the Ley Creek sewer in Syracuse, Roesch Memorial Stadium in Buffalo, and improvements in Bear Mountain Park. It gave electricity to the Pennsylvania Railroad and backed the first diesel engines. In Washington, D.C., it was the WPA that built the zoo, the mall, and the Federal Trade Commission building. In California it built the Camarillo Mental Hospital and the fairgrounds in San Francisco. Fort Knox gold depository in Kentucky was built by the WPA. It built the Bonneville Dam on the Columbia River and Boulder Dam on the Colorado River. In the early days, especially, the WPA distributed food and provided medical and dental care to New Yorkers who otherwise could not have afforded it. In addition, WPA workers indexed, analyzed, surveyed, investigated, and published mountains of data on every conceivable aspect of New York's history and current problems.

How Milwaukee Worked

The City of Milwaukee developed projects for 12,000 workers under WPA financing. They were em-

Persuading the Farmers

Farmers initially were dubious about the central feature of the AAA. Their natural instincts were, as they alway had been for farmers, to attempt to increase production, not limit it. It was pointed out to them that manufacturers did not flood the consumer market with goods, which would have the inevitable effect of driving down prices, but instead regulated their supplies to maximize profits. Farmers may have had their reservations about such theoretical arguments in favor of crop restriction, but as higher prices and subsidies began reaching their pockets, they readily accepted the policy.

ployed in constructing and improving city streets, sewer and water mains, city playgrounds, bridges, and public buildings; modernizing city real-estate tax files and city records; building exhibits and classifying specimens at the Milwaukee Public Museum; and using unemployed doctors and nurses to immunize children.

The Milwaukee County Department of Outdoor Relief certified relief workers for referral to WPA employment, with one employable member (usually the male parent) identified for each case. In 1936 the county reported that about 19,000 relief cases had a worker placed on the WPA. This meant that only about 3,200 families were left on local government relief.

FEDERAL PROJECT ONE

What was known as Federal Project One (often abbreviated to Federal One) was perhaps the aspect of the WPA for which it is best remembered (see Volume 5,

The mighty Bonneville Dam on the Columbia River in Oregon, completed in 1937, was one of the WPA's most ambitious projects.

Chapter 4, "The Arts in the Depression"); its projects mainly had to do with music, writing, theater, and the visual arts, which greatly enriched the cultural life of the nation.

The Federal Theater Project, Federal Music Project, Federal Art Project, and Federal Writers' Project employed actors, painters,

As part of the Federal Art Project, teenagers in New York City are concentrating on the challenge of decorative metalwork.

Wage Power

The Works Progress Administration was Harry Hopkins' final relief program before poor health forced him to step down in 1938. He then became secretary of commerce, a cabinet position, but even so, less taxing than administering the great New Deal agencies. Hopkins insisted that WPA projects be structured so as to maximize the percentage of funding that got into the hands of laborers as wages. He was relentless in his determination to keep down administration expenses.

The Tennessee Valley Authority

Although the Tennessee Valley Authority did not in itself profess to being a job-creation agency, in reality it was. It had originally been conceived as a way of taming and developing the Tennessee River and to create electrical power. The federal government had acquired the site at Muscle Shoals, Alabama, in 1916 with the intention of constructing a dam there. This was never done, and although there was talk of selling the land, Senator George W. Norris of Nebraska fought doggedly throughout the 1920s to keep public control of the property.

By 1933 public opinion was more favorable to government participation in commercial matters, and President Roosevelt was particularly interested in regional planning and conservation. On May 18, 1933, he signed the Tennessee Valley Authority Act. With this the Tennessee Valley Authority became more than just a commission to build a series of dams and transmission lines; it was also charged with responsibility to "provide for the agricultural and industrial development of said valley" and to

Construction of the Wilson Dam, 1923. Named for President Wilson, who acquired the region in 1916, it was completed before the advent of the TVA.

foster "an orderly and physical, economic, and social development of such areas."

It was significant that the TVA was established as a regional authority that transcended state lines. In taking this action, Congress showed a growing awareness for regional and national planning as well as understanding that the particular problems of the Tennessee Valley could not be solved by local governments acting alone. The specific project was to control the water resources by constructing a system of dams. They were designed to maintain a 9-foot navigation channel over a 650-mile length of the river, from Knoxville, Tennessee, to Paducah, Kentucky, to reduce the destruction of floods that had plagued the region for generations. By 1939 the TVA had built four dams and bought a fifth, Hale's Bar Dam, from private interest. The publicly built dams were Wilson Dam (actually finished before the creation of the TVA) and Wheeler Dam (1936) in Alabama, Pickwick Landing Dam (1938) in

As an example of New Deal projects joining forces, CCC recruits from Idaho set out to work on reforestation in Tennessee for the TVA in 1933.

Tennessee, and Norris Dam (1936) on the Clinch River in Tennessee.

The project was also to improve navigation on the Tennessee River, as well as to provide flood control, reforestation, improve marginal farmlands, assist in industrial agricultural development, and create a government nitrate and phosphorus manufacturing facility. The U.S. Department of Agriculture (including the Agricultural Adjustment Administration), the Civilian Conservation Corps, and state agricultural experiment stations and extension services were among the many agencies that joined forces in working with the TVA.

By September 1939 the dams were generating electrical power which was sold wholesale to the local municipalities and cooperative associations of the region to the benefit of 325,000 consumers; along with these communities four large industrial companies were using TVA power. A stipulation of the Tennessee Valley Authority Act was that power was to be sold to its consumers at low rates. Almost 7,000 miles of rural line were in operation on June 30, 1939; most of them were owned and operated by cooperative associations and municipalities, and more than 85 percent of the total construction of new lines carried power to areas previously without electricity. Generally, the Rural Electrification

Flooded farmland in Tennessee in the mid-1930s. Chronic flooding blighted farmers' lives, and to control it was one of the TVA's principal goals.

Administration loaned the capital, and the TVA or some other agency built the lines.

Low-cost electricity and improved phosphates enabled farmers to sustain agriculture and enjoy the modern conveniences that electricity brought (see Volume 3, Chapter 6, "Continuing Plight of the Farmer"). At Norris the authority established an experiment between industry and the inhabitants of the cooperative community, who were trained in various skills. The plan was to provide instruction in crop, garden, poultry, and dairy farming. The men were also taught wood and metalwork. The women received courses in home management.

Also important were the employment opportunities on the construction sites, which had high TVA standards. Originally, workers were employed based on special tests developed in cooperation with the United States Civil Service Commission. They received 45 cents for unskilled labor and $1.00 for skilled labor, regardless of color. On December 5, 1933, the Civil Works Administration allocated $3.3 million to be spent by the TVA. The money allowed the TVA to hire laborers from the relief rolls without qualifying through the special tests. Labor and management worked together on their common problems and job training, which contributed to efficiency and also prepared the employees for future work when the TVA project was finished. By 1936 the TVA held 8,000 job-training meetings attended by 63,000 workers, and 4,000 adult education meetings with 79,120 people attending.

A large audience in a New York park enjoys a performance put on by the Federal Theater Project in the mid-1930s.

musicians, and writers. In 1937 almost 45 percent of all artists were employed by government.

Before the creation of the WPA and the Federal Theater Project various drama units were established in 1934 by Harry Hopkins through an earlier federal agency, the Civil Works Administration. But what is striking about the WPA when compared to other government art projects is the variety of activities, the sheer number of artists employed, and the amount of work produced. Its significance lay not only in the quality of the work but also in the large amount that reached the public. The statistics give a sense of the enormous scope of federal patronage in the 1930s.

The Theater Project

The Theater Project, headed by Hallie Flanagan, employed 12,700 theater workers at its peak, nine out of ten of whom came from the relief rolls. Units were established

in 31 states and New York City, with most states in turn creating more than one company or unit. Federal Theater units gave more than 1,000 performances each month before nearly one million people—78 percent of these audience members were admitted free of charge, many seeing live theater for the first time. The Federal Theater Project produced over 1,200 plays in its four-year history, introducing a hundred new playwrights.

About 50 percent of FTP personnel were actors; the rest were writers, designers, theater musicians, dancers, stage hands, box office staff, ushers, and maintenance workers, as well as accounting and secretarial staff. These workers were employed in theater companies in 40 cities in 22 states. The largest projects were those in New York, Los Angeles, and Chicago.

Stage productions included new plays, classical plays, plays formerly produced on Broadway, modern foreign plays, children's plays, revues and musical comedies, vaudeville, dance productions, American pageants,

and puppet and marionette plays. Units also produced foreign and ethnic works, including Yiddish, African American, Italian, Spanish, French, and German units. The FTP was terminated in 1939 because conservatives in Congress believed it to be dominated by political radicals.

Putting Artists to Work

The first national art project was the Public Works of Art Project, which ran from the winter of 1933 to the spring of 1934 and was directed by Edward Bruce. Unlike the later Federal Art Project, the artists did not have to be certified for relief in order to gain employment on the PWAP. The director in New York City was the head of the Whitney Museum, Juliana Force. The pay scale was between $26.50 and $42.50 per week, and 3,749 artists were employed.

Because of the brief duration of PWAP several of its projects were only started up, but many were continued under the WPA/FAP. One of the most provocative pieces done under PWAP was Isamu Noguchi's *Play Mountain*, the model for the earth sculpture playground that was the predecessor for similar designs being built today in Atlanta and Detroit.

For the artists the Federal Art Project (FAP) provided models, publicity, testing, and research, which produced new and more reliable paint pigments as well as technical services such as framing and restoring. Under Holger Cahill the FAP oversaw major endeavors throughout the country. For example, a mural project executed 2,500 murals in hospitals, schools, and public buildings.

Anton Refregier's sketches for the murals in the Federal Works Agency Building at the 1939 World's Fair symbolize several of these projects. In New York Berenice Abbott's photographs, published in a book entitled *Changing New York,* were turned into guides to the city and the state. The FAP not only created murals, easel paintings, graphics, sculpture, and photographs, but also performed a wide range of services to the artists and to the public. At its peak the Federal Art Project employed 2,323 artists in New York City alone. Between 1935 and 1943 these New Yorkers produced about 200 murals, 2,100 sculptures, over 12,000 easel paintings, 75,000 prints, and an index of about 6,000 American design plates. By 1943 the FAP had probably allocated over 20,000 works in New York City to tax-supported institutions, which were then asked to reimburse the FAP for all nonlabor costs.

Projects took place all over the country, wherever unemployed artists could be found. The cultural impact of this simple fact was far-reaching, summed up by Holger Cahill, director of the Federal Art Project, in a 1939 speech:

"The Project has discovered that such a simple matter as finding employment for the artist in his hometown has been of the greatest importance. It has, for one thing, helped to stem the cultural erosion which in the past two decades has drawn most of America's art talent to a few large cities. It has brought the artist closer to the interests of a public which needs him, and which is now learning to understand him. And it has made the artist more responsive to the inspiration of the country, and through this

Sculptor Augusta Savage with a beautiful example of her work, at the Harlem Art Exhibition in June 1936, arranged by the WPA.

the artist is bringing every aspect of American life into the currency of art."

Music for the Masses

Nikolai Sokoloff, the former director of the Cleveland Symphony, ran the Federal Music Project (FMP). At its peak it had about 16,000 musicians with ensembles—orchestras and chamber groups; choral and opera units; concert, military, and dance bands; and theater orchestras—that performed about 5,000 performances to three million people every week. There were music projects for local com-

posers, schools and colleges, and civic groups. Small admissions charges helped meet costs.

The Federal Music Project also provided classes in rural areas and urban neighborhoods; it is estimated that 132,000 children and adults in 27 states were given weekly music lessons of one sort or another. A Composers Forum Laboratory afforded composers in several major cities the opportunity to hear their work performed with complete instrumentation. The Index of American Composers, similar to the Design Index, catalogued 5,500 works by 1,500 composers; and all of them

Poster Art

As part of the Federal Arts Project the Works Progress Administration established the Poster Division in 1935. The Poster Division was a successful attempt to provide work for unemployed commercial artists—often looked down on for the nature of their work but in fact containing within their ranks top-quality artists and designers. The famous French artist Henri de Toulouse-Lautrec at the end of the 19th century created posters that are as well-loved and prized as any painting of the period.

A poster is simply a publicly displayed announcement of an event, program, or product designed to communicate its message at a glance. Its most common application has been as an advertising medium; and in the 1930s, before the days of television, the poster was unrivaled for its impact-making ability. Poster design was by then a highly skilled profession, where the artists/designers would apply their disciplined use of color and composition, combined with an understanding of modern printing techniques, in particular offset lithography, to the client's requirements.

The Poster Division took talented young commercial artists and designers off the unemployment rolls and gave them a chance to show off their skills, and the fruits of their work rank among the most memorable visual records of the 1930s and

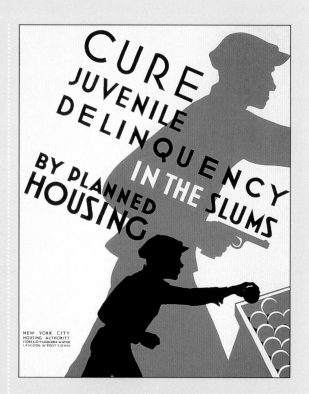

A powerful poster drawing attention to the antisocial consequences of poor housing, produced by the Federal Art Project in 1936.

This WPA poster produced in the 1930s promotes a solution to the problem of high infant mortality among slum-dwellers.

specifically of the New Deal and its projects. For example, it seemed natural for the various New Deal agencies to advertise their programs with WPA posters.

In New York by the end of the 1930s nearly 600,000 posters for various governmental agencies, from federal down to municipal, had been printed under WPA auspices. Posters were displayed in libraries and museums, and many received high critical acclaim.

In 1938 the art critic Sydney Kellner praised "the amazing design quality invested in these posters which has raised them to the status of a true art form." He went on to say that the scorn traditionally heaped on commercial artists by "fine" artists "seems to have been swept away completely by the constant barrage of good posters turned out by the WPA/Federal Art Project."

were performed by the FMP musical ensembles. Extensive recording of folk music was carried out, especially in the Southeast and Southern regions of the country. The WPA members pioneered in experimental music therapy.

The Federal Writers' Project

The Federal Writers' Project (FWP), headed by Henry Alsberg, employed 6,686 writers at its peak in April 1936 and had projects in all existing 48 states and the District of Columbia. By October 1941 it had produced 3.5 million copies of 800 titles.

The FWP is best known for its American Guide Series. The purpose of the series was to create comprehensive guidebooks for every state and protectorate; similar guides were published for smaller localities. Each guide included detailed descriptions of towns and villages, historic sites, and other points of interest. They were often accompanied by collections of oral history and folklore, essays about local life, photographs, and other artwork.

To this day the American Guide Series constitutes the most comprehensive encyclopedia of Americana ever published; several volumes have been reissued recently, some in updated form.

Other activities of the Federal Writers' Project included studies on such topics as architecture, science for children, and the Native Americans. Among the most important are the oral history archives created by FWP workers, including priceless archives like the Slave Narratives and collections of folklore. They contained the life histories of the ex-slaves, giving dimension and texture to 19th-century life in the African American community. In addition to

working on FWP projects, writers provided research, writing, and editorial services to other government agencies.

THE END OF THE NEW DEAL

The numbers of people given work under the New Deal were vast: four million were employed by the CWA in 1932 to 1933, five million by the WPA from 1935 to 1938. Such projects represented a massive extension of federal intervention in the economic and social life of the country. For the most part Americans approved of this seismic change. And such was the momentum created by the Roosevelt administration that the essentials of the New Deal were in place almost before anyone had time to reflect on what was happening.

Nevertheless, despite economic improvement, the New Deal had not succeeed in driving the Great Depression from the land. The worst was behind, but FDR had no illusions that recovery was assured. In January 1935 he referred in his annual address to unfinished business and committed himself to a comprehensive social security program along with an expanded program of public works. In the year and a half leading up to his reelection campaign in 1936 President Roosevelt would throw his energies into extending the New Deal—in what historians refer to as the second New Deal.

Poster for a WPA exhibition in 1938. The Index of American Design comprised 20,000 renditions of American decorative art from earliest times.

—— SEE ALSO ——

◆ Volume 2, Chapter 2, The First Hundred Days

◆ Volume 2, Chapter 6, The Election of 1936

◆ Volume 3, Chapter 2, Shadow over the Countryside

◆ Volume 4, Chapter 5, Welfare

◆ Volume 5, Chapter 4, The Arts in the Depression

THE ELECTION OF 1936

The presidential election of 1936 was the public's judgment on the New Deal. Despite heavy criticism of Roosevelt and his policies from both the political left and right, he won a landslide victory and, in so doing, changed the makeup of American party politics.

At the end of President Franklin D. Roosevelt's first term critics and supporters alike reflected on his first four years in office. In terms of introducing legislation Roosevelt had accomplished much. In the famed Hundred Days after he took office in 1933 Congress had passed 15 major pieces of legislation (see Chapter 2, "The First Hundred Days"); there had never been such a concentrated period of legislative activity in U.S. political history. In the intervening years FDR had put in place more elements of the New Deal he had promised when he came to power (see Chapter 1, "The Election of 1932"). They included, for example, the Social Security Act of 1935.

Problems remained, however. Unemployment was still consistently high. An estimated 10 million persons were still without jobs. Critics from both right and left attacked Roosevelt—the right because his reforms went too far,

Roosevelt prepares to make a radio broadcast in 1937, putting him in touch directly with millions of ordinary Americans.

Why Hate FDR?

Roosevelt has gone down in history as one of America's best-loved presidents. He was also one of the most hated. FDR's enemies, the most implacable of whom were among the privileged and wealthy, loathed the man they saw as a traitor to his—and their—class. They could not even speak his name, calling him "That man in the White House." They saw the social and economic changes he proposed as threats to their power, influence, and not least, income. In the mansions of Manhattan's Fifth Avenue, the gentlemen's clubs, and the boardrooms of big business FDR was *persona non grata*.

1932 contest against the despised Herbert Hoover. The turnout was high because FDR attracted millions of new voters. Political historians point to the 1936 election as a watershed in contemporary politics. The race defined party positions for the next 50-plus years. Roosevelt's overwhelming victory reflected popular opinion that he had charted a course for recovery.

1. CRITICS OF THE PRESIDENT

The election campaign of 1936 arrayed the critics of the New Deal against Roosevelt. There were many on both the political right and the left. On the right Republicans and conservative Democrats aligned themselves with business interests to oppose what they perceived as Roosevelt's assault on the capitalist free-market economy and the supplanting of states' rights by

federal intervention. On the left charismatic populist leaders, socialists, and labor organizers complained that the New Deal had not gone far enough. Handed the opportunity to change the United States fundamentally and forever, they argued, FDR had missed his chance.

American socialists, for example, saw his program of legislation as propping up capitalism rather than trying to fundamentally restructure it. Conservative coalitions, on the other hand, including the American Liberty League—whose membership included financiers, industrialists, corporate lawyers, and conservative Democrats—saw New Deal components such as the National Industrial Recovery Act of 1933 as undermining the economic stability of the country (see Volume 4, Chapter 4, "The Right-Wing Backlash," and Volume 5, Chapter 1, "Government, Industry, and

the left because they did not go far enough. If the New Deal did not work in one term, critics from both sides contended, then it would not work in two.

In 1936 the American public gave their opinion on Roosevelt's progress. Overwhelmingly they approved of what he had accomplished. FDR won the election with 60.8 percent of the popular vote, up from 57.4 percent in the

At his 52nd birthday party in January 1934 Roosevelt mocked critics who accused him of becoming too dictatorial by dressing up as as a Roman dictator. Among the women in his court are his wife Eleanor and his daughter Anna.

Economic Policy"). The first National Labor Relations Board (NLRB), established in 1935, enforced collective bargaining agreements as provided for in the act. Business leaders increasingly viewed government policy as unsound, irrational, and socially threatening. In particular they were disturbed by some of the people who worked for FDR, seeing them as being inherently antibusiness and against free enterprise.

THE SUPREME COURT

The end of Roosevelt's first term was also affected by growing conflict with the Supreme Court. In 1934 the Court had begun ruling New Deal legislation unconstitutional. By 1936 it had invalidated six key pieces of legislation. They included the National Industrial Recovery Act, the Railroad Retirement Act, and the Agricultural Adjustment Act (AAA). Roosevelt contended that the conservatives on the Court were invalidating perfectly constitutional laws and that their interpretation was flawed and out of step with the times.

Roosevelt's frustration with the Supreme Court and his intention to prevent it from what he saw as interference earned the suspicion of many people, including numerous members of his own Democratic Party. They feared that the president would try to reinforce the position of the executive at the cost of that of the Supreme Court.

In a speech entitled "Shall We Plow under the Supreme Court?" American Liberty League president Jowett Shouse defended the Court's actions against what he considered Roosevelt's illegitimate attacks on the Constitution: "Now what have we seen these last two years? An emergency? Oh, yes. I grant you there was an emergency, a serious emergency, but I do not grant that it was any more serious than the emergency in the time of the World War. But under this administration, not one, not two, but literally dozens of bills, the authorship of which in many instances is wholly unknown, have been sent down from the White House to the committees of Congress with instructions that they be passed overnight without the change in the dot of an 'i' or the cross of a 't,' without amendment and without debate. Even the chairmen of the committees who have received them and have presented them and

Republican Democrats? John J. Raskob (left) and Jowett Shouse were influential conservative Democrats who founded the anti-FDR American Liberty League.

in whose names they have appeared as legislative enactments haven't known what was in the bills. That is the kind of legislation you have been having since the spring of 1933."

FDR TALKS TO THE PEOPLE

Roosevelt left Americans to judge for themselves his efforts and the progress of his administration. Although other politicians and speech writers have extravagantly

Making His Case

Roosevelt was a highly skilled self-publicist and was always ready to use press conferences or radio broadcasts to get his message across to the voters. The case he put before the people in his election campaign had one of its clearest expressions months earlier, in his 1935 State of the Union address. Roosevelt insisted that the New Deal programs were working and that 1934 had been a better year for all Americans. He also tried to lay out his attitude toward America's wealthy.

"We have...a clear mandate from the people, that Americans must forswear that conception of the acquisition of wealth, which, through excessive profits, creates undue private power over private affairs and, to our misfortune, over public affairs as well. In building toward this end we do not destroy ambition, nor do we seek to divide our wealth into equal shares on stated occasions. We continue to recognize the greater ability of some to earn more than others. But we do assert that the ambition of the individual to obtain for him and his a proper security, a reasonable leisure, and a decent living throughout life is an ambition to be preferred to the appetite for great wealth and great power. ...

"The ledger of the past year shows many more gains than losses. Let us not forget that, in addition to saving millions from utter destitution, child labor has been for the moment outlawed, thousands of homes saved to their owners, and, most important of all, the morale of the Nation has been restored. Viewing the year 1934 as a whole, you and I can agree that we have a generous measure of reasons for giving thanks.

"It is not empty optimism that moves me to a strong hope for the coming year. We can, if we will, make 1935 a genuine period of good feeling, sustained by a sense of purposeful progress. Beyond the material recovery, I sense a spiritual recovery as well. The people of America are turning as never before to those permanent values that are not limited to the physical objectives of life. There are growing signs of this on every hand. In the face of these spiritual impulses we are sensible of the divine Providence to which nations can turn now, as always, for guidance and fostering care."

borrowed the idea, Roosevelt in one of his 1934 Fireside Chats asked Americans to use one simple test: self-examination. "Are you better off than you were last year? Are your debts less burdensome? Is your bank account more secure? Are your working conditions better? Is your faith in your own individual future more

A cartoon from 1934 shows FDR as a doctor trying a whole range of remedies to cure Uncle Sam. Critics of the New Deal charged that it was fragmentary and opportunistic, supporters that it was an appropriate reaction to the economic emergency.

firmly grounded?" he said. "I have no question in my mind as to what your answer will be. The record is written in the experiences of your own personal lives."

OPPOSITION FROM THE LEFT

While many to Roosevelt's right believed the president's social programs and push for a strong federal government were moving the country toward communism, the American radical left considered the president's modest attempts at wealth distribution to

Ida Fuller was the first person in the United States to receive welfare under the terms of the Social Security Act of 1935.

be sorely deficient. While right-wing critics considered Roosevelt a class traitor, those on the left considered him faithful to his aristocratic origins. Though a

•

"The great betrayer and liar, Franklin D. Roosevelt…"

•

vibrant Socialist Party and radical workers' movement had existed earlier in the century, their charismatic leaders were now either dead or deported. While some Americans were still attracted by international communism and socialism, it was home-grown populism that would gain major momentum prior to the elections of 1936. Activists such as Dr. Francis E. Townsend, Huey Long, and Father Charles Coughlin connected with poorer Americans with their contentions that the New Deal did not go far enough. While these men were opponents of Soviet-style communism, they recaptured the mantle of American-style populism and mutualism to criticize modern capitalism and preach the idea of greater wealth distribution.

Coughlin was a Catholic priest whose highly politicized radio program held immense sway among Depression-era listeners. At the height of his popularity roughly a third of the nation listened to his calls for radical economic and social reform. At

first a passionate Roosevelt supporter, Coughlin soon turned against the president and became more extreme in his political views.

Coughlin founded a national movement, called the National Union for Social Justice, that advocated the nationalization of banks, national resources, and utilities, and proposed monetary reform measures. Despite the priest's later sympathies for right-wing dictators like Adolf Hitler and Benito Mussolini, his critique of capitalism brought to public discourse ideas considerably to the left of Roosevelt's.

While Roosevelt would be remembered for bringing about the Social Security Administration, the so-called Townsendites, and their demands for old-age pensions, were a more radical force in the direction of social protection for senior citizens. Dr. Francis E. Townsend, a retired physician, advocated a 2 percent sales tax to provide American seniors with a

Coughlin Attacks FDR

"The great betrayer and liar, Franklin D. Roosevelt, who promised to drive the money changers from the temple, had succeeded [only] in driving the farmers from their homesteads and the citizens from their homes in the cities. I ask you to purge the man who claims to be a Democrat from the Democratic Party, and I mean Franklin Double-Crossing Roosevelt."

"Our Government still upholds one of the worst evils of decadent capitalism, namely, that production must be only at a profit for the owners, for the capitalist, and not for the laborer," said Coughlin. "This philosophy of finance, or of distribution of profits, based on the theory of 'pay-while-you-work' for the laborer can only be identified with destruction of the entire system of capitalism."

Public works projects, like this one in New Jersey, were condemned by the right for increasing dependence on the federal government.

$200 monthly income. By 1936 there were some two million Townsend Club members.

HUEY LONG

A major threat to FDR's reelection came from Huey Long, former governor of and now senator from Louisiana (see Volume 4, Chapter 3, "Huey Long"). Long, a Democrat, was a flamboyant speaker with an acidic sense of humor. As governor of one the nation's poorest states, he took on Louisiana's feudal system, attacking big oil interests and investing heavily in public infrastructure and education. Louisiana's poor whites practically worshiped Long, though critics saw in the charismatic leader and his strong-arm tactics a down-home version of Mussolini. When Long was elected to the Senate, he became perhaps the strongest voice of dissent on the left, directly challenging Roosevelt and the New Deal. "Only one political

The dapper figure of Huey Long, known as the Louisiana Kingfish. Long's flamboyance and rhetoric lent great appeal to his Share-Our-Wealth message.

Long Attacks FDR

Huey Long used a radio broadcast in January 1935 to accuse the president of going back on his promise of the redistribution of wealth: "Hundreds of words were used by Mr. Roosevelt to make these promises to the people, but they were made over and over again. He reiterated these pledges even after he took his oath as President. Summed up, what these promises meant was: 'Share our wealth.'

"When I saw him spending all his time of ease and recreation with the business partners of Mr. John D. Rockefeller, Jr., with such men as the Astors, etc., maybe I ought to have had better sense than to have believed he would ever break down their big fortunes to give enough to the masses to end poverty—maybe some will think me weak for ever believing it all, but millions of other people were fooled the same as myself. I was like a drowning man grabbing at a straw, I guess. The face and eyes, the hungry forms of mothers and children, the aching hearts of students denied education were before our eyes, and when Roosevelt promised, we jumped for that ray of hope.

"So therefore I call upon the men and women of America to immediately join in our work and movement to share our wealth."

Dr. Francis E. Townsend explains his old-age pension plan in Philadelphia in 1936. By then the Social Security Act had made his plan largely redundant.

opponent ever struck a chord of fear in President Franklin Roosevelt and that was Governor, and then Senator Huey Long," says historian James Hume.

Long's Share-Our-Wealth plan, a third way between communism and capitalism, appealed to millions of poor Americans. Where Roosevelt was accused of being soft on the economic elite, Long promised to put a limit on and tax major fortunes and to redistribute that money to the nation's poor in the form of guaranteed minimum incomes, old-age pensions, and shorter work days. By 1935 the Share-Our-Wealth Society boasted 27,000 clubs with more than seven million members. In August that year Long announced his intent to run for the presidency, if not as a Democrat, then as a third-party candidate. He wrote a "second autobiography" chronicling his first hundred days in office. While

the polls showed nothing near a Long victory, it was feared that he might win upward of 10 percent of the popular vote, splitting the Democratic vote and allowing a Republican victory. A month later Long was assassinated.

THE DEMOCRATS IN 1935

Roosevelt faced significant dissent from within the Democratic Party. Some conservative Democrats—including the former presidential candidate Al Smith and business

leaders John J. Raskob and Pierre S. DuPont—organized themselves under the banner of the American Liberty League (see Volume 4, Chapter 1, "Left vs. Right"). Believing the New Deal represented too much government intervention in U.S. life, the league reportedly spent more than the Republicans in denouncing it. They even considered nominating Georgia governor Eugene Talmage as president. The man was well known for his virulent racism.

Roosevelt also faced criticism from conservative Southern Democrats, typified by his vice president John N. Garner. Garner had been valuable to Roosevelt from the outset, first as the tie-breaking vote in his nomination for president and later as a supporter of the New Deal reforms, albeit a somewhat reluctant one. By 1934 Garner was becoming increasingly upset about his lack of involvement in daily affairs. He complained that his post was "not worth a pitcher of warm spit." He and his wife intentionally kept away from the social whirl in the capital, attending functions only when obliged to do so, and preferring instead to return to Texas when they could.

The Second New Deal

The second New Deal of 1935 was neither as far-ranging nor as revolutionary as either Roosevelt or his opponents presented it. Some of the major pieces of legislation are listed below:

April 8	Emergency Relief Appropriation Act
April 27	Soil Conservation Act
May 6	Works Progress Administration (executive order)
July 5	National Labor Relations (Wagner) Act
August 14	Social Security Act
August 28	Public Utility Holding Company Act
August 29	Farm Mortgage Moratorium Act (1935)
August 30	Revenue Act of 1935

Like many other Southern Democrats, Garner disliked much of the New Deal legislation. Tensions increased when Roosevelt accused him of leaking details of cabinet meetings. The president went so far as to refuse to discuss key subjects until Garner had left the room.

Roosevelt also faced disapproval from within his own family. Theodore Roosevelt, Jr., son of former president Theodore Roosevelt, FDR's fifth cousin and role model, felt marginalized by the president and first lady in the 1930s. He saw the president as becoming an American version of the Italian dictator Mussolini. Theodore Jr., and to some degree his brothers, became the focus for much of the opposition to the New Deal; they denounced FDR as "a maverick who does not have the brand of our family."

2. THE SECOND NEW DEAL

Partly in response to the challenge from the populists and partly to satisfy those in his own party calling for more reform, Roosevelt appeared in 1935 to lean further toward the left. It was also partly a reaction to the decision of the Supreme Court to rule illegal the NRA, the linchpin of the New Deal. In a burst of energy FDR launched what he and his advisers dubbed the second New Deal.

The legislation FDR backed in 1935 included the Social Security Act, which provided old-age pensions and unemployment insurance (see Volume 4, Chapter 5, "Welfare"); a certain amount of tax reform, including a tax on profits businesses had not distributed to their shareholders; and the National Labor Relations Act, sometimes called the Wagner Act for its sponsor, New York senator

Robert Wagner. The Emergency Relief Appropriation Act increased funds for the job-creation schemes of the Public Works Administration

•

"…a maverick who does not have the brand of our family…"

•

In May FDR created the Works Progress Administration. The WPA was conceived as another way to sponsor public works projects, ranging from construction to Federal One, which sponsored the arts and culture.

How the right portrayed FDR: This 1937 cartoon shows a man struggling under the burden of taxes to finance the New Deal. The tax burden actually rose comparatively little for most Americans.

Although business interests strongly opposed the legislation of the second New Deal, it was generally not as harmful to them as they claimed. The tax measure did not actually cost them very much. The Social Security Act was relatively limited in its cost simply because it excluded millions of Americans, including, for example, many farmers and domestic servants. And the collective bargaining reinforced by the National Labor Relations Act (NLRA) actually helped business regularize its relations with unions. The NLRA was largely a more coherent piece of industrial legislation to replace

Roosevelt supporters welcome his renomination at the Democratic Convention in Philadelphia on June 26, 1936.

the wealth, privilege, and influence he had come to believe were putting obstacles in the way of reform. The attack would culminate in his nomination speech at the 1936 Democratic National Convention, when he condemned those he labeled "economic royalists" (see box, opposite).

The second New Deal, like the first, was never going to satisfy everyone. Both liberal and conservative commentators of the day accused Roosevelt of showing that he stood for nothing beyond his own reelection. Many of his most popular ideas, they claimed, were stolen from his opponents. He was personally untrustworthy.

It was not the first or last time FDR would be accused of legislating without a commitment to any central philosophy or vision. *The Economist*, in a long survey of the New Deal in October 1936, had described the National Industrial Recovery Act as "an extraordinary catch-all [that] collects more divergent economic and social theories under the roof of a single enactment than any other piece of legislation ever known."

Other commentators see the second New Deal as a skillfully crafted platform designed to fend off challenges from both right and left. In this interpretation FDR cleverly positioned himself as, above all, an adaptable politician.

what the Supreme Court had struck down. It gave employees the right to organize and also made employers enter into collective bargaining discussions with unions. The act created a stronger form of the National Labor Relations Board, or NLRB, which continues to function today. This body was charged with overseeing the laws created under the act and

being sure its provisions were enforced properly.

The second New Deal had the effect of widening the gap between Roosevelt and his critics on the right. In this second phase of his reforms FDR deliberately abandoned the inclusivity of his earlier policies, which had depended on achieving a unity of all sections of society, to launch an attack on

Roosevelt signs the National Labor Relations Act of 1935 as labor organizers study images of strike violence in this memorial painting. The act, and other prolabor legislation, earned FDR the suspicion of business interests.

Economic Royalists

Roosevelt's acceptance speech after he had been nominated as presidential candidate at the Democratic National Convention in June 1936 set out his agenda for the campaign to come. After looking back at the achievements of his first term, the president went on to launch an attack on what he called "economic royalists." Those people, dynasties, and corporations, he went on, had gained unacceptable power in the United States by the "concentration of control over material things." This was, he remarked, a form of economic tyranny. The speech heralded a new direction for the second term. Instead of seeking to maintain as broad an appeal as possible, Roosevelt attacked one special interest group in order to garner the support of another group with particular reformist, social, and liberal sympathies. The assault on concentrated economic power was reminiscent of attacks around the turn of the 20th century on the gigantic trusts that dominated U.S. business. It also alienated FDR even more from America's business leaders and the rich.

POLITICAL POSITIONS

The campaign of 1936 was highly ideologically charged. The two major political parties each shaped distinct policies that would divide and distinguish them throughout the 20th century. Both parties also abandoned long-held ideas. The Democrats, with their reliance on the Southern vote, had traditionally been the party advocating states' rights but were now supporting federal welfare and social policies. The Republicans had pressed for an extension of federal powers in the past, but now shifted to militating for local and state rights.

THE CONVENTION

Despite opposition within his own party, Roosevelt was nominated at the 1936 Democratic National Convention in Philadelphia. It was

one of the few occasions when the president's handicap was publicly displayed. Supported by two men on the way to the podium, he reached out to shake hands with one of the crowd. His leg brace snapped, and he fell to the ground, the pages of his speech

scattered on the floor. "Clean me up," he said to the people surrounding him as he brushed off the dirt and was helped to his feet. Few people were aware of the incident. FDR went on to make a speech that enthralled millions of Americans nationwide listening live on the radio: "Governments can err, presidents do make mistakes, but the immortal Dante tells us that divine justice weighs the sins of the cold-blooded and the sins of the warm-hearted in different scales. Better the occasional faults of a government that lives in a spirit of charity than the consistent omissions of a government frozen in the ice of its own indifference."

Months later FDR wound up his presidential campaign at New York City's Madison Square Garden. There he launched an attack on business interests and his other opponents, the sheer violence of which led even many of his supporters to begin to question the wisdom of his antagonism toward the business community. "Never before in all our history have these

FDR makes his acceptance speech at the 1936 Democratic Convention; he said that Americans had a "rendezvous with destiny."

Roosevelt's Black Cabinet

Mary McLeod Bethune, one of the most prominent members of the Black Cabinet, photographed at her desk during World War II.

A significant component of the Roosevelt administration's 1936 success across racial and economic lines can be attributed to the black support FDR—and, more conspicuously, Eleanor Roosevelt—courted for the Democratic Party. Roosevelt himself was sometimes reluctant to make antiracist gestures that might offend the Southern Democrats on whose support he relied, but early in his administration he openly sought the advice of black leaders. He appointed a significantly higher proportion of black Americans to administrative positions, though not to the highest levels of the administration. Although they were never a formal grouping, they sometimes called themselves the Federal Council on Negro Affairs; the press called them the "Black Cabinet."

Among the most prominent members of the Black Cabinet were Mary McLeod Bethune, a noted educator who served as the National Youth Administration's director of Negro Affairs, at whose home the group often met; William H. Hastie, assistant secretary to the interior department, who became the first black federal judge in 1937; Eugene K. Jones, executive secretary of the National Urban League; Robert L. Vann, editor of *The Pittsburgh Courier*; and Robert C. Weaver, a noted economist who worked for the Public Works Administration. Weaver also worked with Henry Hunt in the Farm Credit Administration, Forrester B. Washington in the Federal Emergency Relief Administration (FERA), and Lawrence A. Axley in the Department of Labor.

Mary McLeod Bethune began her career as a Florida schoolteacher and founded a school that eventually became Bethune–Cookman College. She was active in the National Council of Negro Women as well as the National Youth Administration and was a confidante of Eleanor Roosevelt.

Many of the members of the Black Cabinet were notable in their own right. William Henry Hastie was a lawyer, educator, and public official. He was the first African American appointed to the U.S. Court of Appeals. He was also dean of law at Howard University from 1939 to 1946 and governor of the Virgin Islands from 1946 to 1949.

Eugene K. Jones organized the National Urban League and served as its executive director from 1918 to 1941. He was Negro Affairs adviser to the U.S. Department of Commerce from 1933 to 1943. He served as the chairman of Negro advisory committees for the Texas Centennial Exposition of 1936 and New York World's Fair of 1939, and later joined the Fair Employment Board of the U.S. Civil Service Commission.

Robert Clifton Weaver was a Harvard-educated Ph.D. who began a distinguished career in public service in 1933 as an aide to Interior Secretary Harold Ickes. He was the first African American appointed to head a federal department, although that would not occur until the administration of Lyndon B. Johnson in the 1960s. He was appointed to the U.S. Housing Authority and War Production Board, and taught at Columbia Teacher's College and New York University School of Education and Hunter College.

The *New York Times* described Weaver as "an expert behind-the-scenes strategist in the civil rights movement," whose motto was "Fight hard and legally, and don't blow your top." The headquarters of the Department of Housing and Urban Development was named for Weaver.

Robert L. Vann was best known as the editor and publisher of *The Pittsburgh Courier*, one of the leading black newspaper in the 1930s; he was also a lawyer. Phyllis T. Garland, a reporter and editor on the paper, noted that Vann "used the paper to further his own career and also to help black people, in tandem."

Most blacks—more than 75 percent lived in the South, but many were disfranchised and could not vote—had been Republicans up until the 1930s, but Vann judged their changing mood. "At one point he decided that the black people were being taken for granted by the Republican Party, which was the party of Lincoln in the black community. And he decided that the time had come for them to become

•

"...he said he saw millions of black people turning Lincoln's picture to the wall."

•

Democrats. This was 1932. The country is in the middle of a depression and there were opportunities not only for black people, but for himself, he thought. So he gave a speech in Cleveland where...he said he saw millions of black people turning Lincoln's picture to the wall. This became a rallying cry for blacks to leave the Republican Party and to become Democrats."

Robert C. Weaver would later record how the group worked. "[T]he Black Cabinet did not have white participants; it had no official standing and kept no minutes. The meetings of the group continued on an irregular schedule, but we were always subject to being called in an emergency.

President Lyndon B. Johnson presents a commission of office to Robert C. Weaver, when he became the first African American cabinet member in January 1966.

"The Black Cabinet provided a forum where problems could be discussed and potential solutions developed.... The members often made concrete decisions and carried out assignments concerning matters such as preparing memoranda for future meetings, presenting ideas to government officials or black leaders, and assembling information for release to the press."

How effective the Black Cabinet was in shaping policy is a matter of debate. Bethune's friendship with Eleanor Roosevelt was a useful informal way to exercise some influence on policy decisions. Roosevelt himself stopped short of fully championing civil rights. He knew he had to keep Southern white voters happy and, despite pressure, failed to support antilynching legislation. There were also inequalities in the distribution of federal assistance (see Volume 5, Chapter 2, "Equality for Some"): In 1935 black Americans, who were about one-tenth of the population, made up about one-sixth of the Americans on relief. Many refused to call themselves Democrats—fewer than 45 percent in 1937—but far more were prepared to vote for Roosevelt, believing that although he did little directly to improve their lot, he offered opportunity and hope.

Charles Coughlin makes a radio broadcast. He bade a tearful farewell to his audience after the defeat in the 1936 election.

forces been so united against one candidate as they stand today. They are unanimous in their hate for me—and I welcome their hatred. I should like to have it said of my first administration that in it the forces of selfishness and of lust for power met their match…. I should like to have it said of my second administration that in it these forces met their master."

THE UNION PARTY

The Union Party was created by the same populists who, disenchanted with New Deal politics, had helped push Roosevelt to the left in the second New Deal. Its leaders included Coughlin, Townsend, and Gerald Smith, the radical Disciples of Christ minister who succeeded Huey Long as leader of the Share-Our-Wealth movement. Smith was a powerful orator who habitually ended his political rallies with a prayer that echoed the words of his predecessor: "Lift us out of this wretchedness, O Lord, out of this poverty, lift us who stand here in slavery tonight…out of the land of bondage into the land of milk and honey where every man is a king but no one wears a crown."

Coughlin chose William Lemke (1878–1950) for the Union Party slate as well as his running mate, Thomas C. O'Brien, a union lawyer from Massachusetts. Lemke was from Fargo, North Dakota, and had served as North Dakota state attorney general and U.S. Representative before he ran for the presidency. He had become bitter toward Roosevelt after FDR had fought against measures Lemke proposed to relieve farm bankruptcy. After Lemke announced his candidacy, reporters were quick to joke that the party convention was held in a phone booth, with Coughlin on the other end of the line.

Jonathan Mitchell, journalist with the *New Republic*, likened Union Party meetings to revival meetings: "They indulged in cries, shrieks, moans, rolling of the eyes and brandishing of the arms that—performed in their own family circles—would have caused their relatives to summon ambulances."

It was ultimately Coughlin's stumping that gained coverage from the news media rather than Lemke's oration, and it was unwelcome attention at that, including a scuffle with a reporter in Boston. The campaign was a bitter one as Lemke and, especially, Coughlin ranted against FDR and his advisers as communists. Lemke noted of the president, "Communist leaders have laid their eggs in his Democratic nest."

Despite some concern that the Union Party would steal votes from Roosevelt in certain areas and shift the election in favor of the Republicans, Lemke even failed to get on the ballot in many states. Coughlin had sworn that he would never speak on the air again if Lemke got fewer than nine million votes. When Lemke got only a tenth of that number, Coughlin did indeed go off the air, saying that "President Roosevelt can be a dictator if he wants to"; he disbanded the Union Party the day after the election.

THE REPUBLICANS

The Republicans were weakened by trouble in their ranks. They had been defeated soundly in the 1934 Congressional elections, which left the Democrats with increased numbers in Congress and the Republicans with the affiliation of only seven state governors. With no strong leader wanting to challenge FDR, the field was wide open. Several candidates were proposed before the convention, held in June. They included Senator William E. Borah of Idaho and Frank Lowden, former governor of Illinois.

Instead the nomination went to Alf Landon of Kansas, the only Republican elected to a gubernatorial post in the 1934 pro-Roosevelt atmosphere. He was said to be "guileless and lacking in color." Landon's running mate was Frank Knox, a Chicago newspaper publisher who had served with Teddy Roosevelt as a Roughrider and had fought in World War I. He viewed the New Deal as akin to creeping communism. That the Republican platform condemned both FDR and the New Deal gained it the support of conservative Democrats. The Republicans spent an estimated $14.2 million on their campaign.

The *New Republic* reported in August 1935 that popular support leaned in favor of Roosevelt "against the outrageous Republican alternative," but also noted "a growing and substantial dissatisfaction because of the meager results that have followed his magnificent promises, and because of the confusion and lack of direction that his rapidly shifting and self-contradictory program embodies."

FDR's Voters
Undeterred by those assailing his political reputation, Roosevelt launched his campaign. He was able to build a coalition consisting of varied ethnic, religious, and geographic groups united by their opposition to intervention by elitist Republicans in business and finance. Among them were millions of America's poor urban dwellers, who often had not bothered to vote, and the traditionally conservative Democrats of the South. FDR met with a positive

reception in the South. *The Atlanta Journal* noted that in a November 1935 visit by Roosevelt to Georgia, public reception was overwhelmingly positive. To great popular support FDR "promised still further progress along the road to economic recovery, gradual reduction of the national budget, and continued consideration for the welfare of the masses of the people."

3. THE CAMPAIGN
Party managers wanted Roosevelt to run a low-key campaign from Washington that would hide his paralysis from the public. Roosevelt had other ideas. He overruled them and set out on a 13,000-mile campaign tour from the East Coast to the West and back again. The strategy allowed FDR both to see for himself conditions in the country after half a decade of depression and to impress voters with his charm and affable personality.

Roosevelt was also careful to court the press to ensure the most

positive reports of his campaign. He took his cue from Al Smith, who in the 1928 presidential campaign had outfitted his "Ballyhoo Train" with a Pullman car that offered all the amenities of a contemporary city room, including typewriters, darkroom, and telegraphy capabilities. The "Roosevelt Special" took the idea further, adding 12 cars to the train, including sleeping accommodations.

The reporters on the train with Roosevelt had unprecedented access to the candidate. He talked and joked with them; once, when a correspondent narrowly missed the train, the president wrote his copy for him until he could catch up. FDR's technique was important: Around 80 to 85 percent of newspaper publishers strongly opposed him, but his relations with the reporters helped ensure fairer coverage of his campaign.

Landon's Campaign
Although Alf Landon was a moderate, fellow Republicans urged him to take an extremely

Roosevelt campaigning in Wilkes-Barre, PA, in October 1936. The campaign trail led him across the United States and back again.

Alf Landon, the Republican presidential candidate, seemed to accept that he had no answer to the popularity of Roosevelt.

conservative position against the New Dealers. Landon's slogan on the campaign trail was "We must drive the spenders out!" In addition to railing against the Democrats for unsound fiscal policy, Landon also attacked them for failing to solve unemployment and Roosevelt specifically for overstepping his bounds as outlined in the Constitution. Landon had the backing of the influential newspaper mogul William Randolph Hearst (see box, opposite).

Landon later reflected on the 1936 election in a brief *U.S. News & World Report* article in 1984. At the start of the convention, he recalled, delegates were "pretty much in favor of Senator Arthur Vandenberg of Michigan, and I sent my campaign manager off to ask if he would accept the vice-president nomination. He was

nowhere to be found.... We were down to the last half-hour and still no No. 2 for the ticket. So we announced that Colonel Knox, whom I had met and liked, was our choice. We hadn't been able to find him, either. Afterward, Knox asked if I was sure I wanted him, and I said certainly. I didn't tell him about Vandenberg. Things were a lot more spontaneous back then.

"Mrs. Landon wasn't active in the 1936 campaign. She told me if I really needed her, she would go with me. But the kids, Nancy and

The New York Times of November 4, 1936, announces the presidential election result most Americans had long expected: a Roosevelt victory by a landslide.

William Randolph Hearst

Among Roosevelt's most implacable right-wing opponents was William Randolph Hearst (1863-1951), one of America's richest men and most controversial publishers. The national newspaper empire Hearst had built from 1891 to the 1920s made him a powerful voice in the affairs of the country, including the debate over Roosevelt's presidency. As early as 1898 Hearst's inflammatory stories had been a contributory factor in whipping up public opinion to support the Spanish–American War, the starting of which he sometimes took credit for.

The desire to influence national affairs remained with Hearst. He launched a political career as a Democrat in 1900 but failed to win high office; before and during World War I his support for the Germans finished any chance of political success. Instead, he played a key part at the Democratic convention of 1931, transferring his support for John Garner to Roosevelt after the third ballot; Garner would become vice president.

Although Hearst originally supported the New Deal, he grew wary of policies that threatened business regulation, rights for labor, and increased taxes. As a result of the Depression the press baron lost a large part of his fortune and had to sell some newspapers and amalgamate others. In 1935 he instructed his editors to start referring to the New Deal as the "raw deal." Following the frustration of Roosevelt's victory in 1936, Hearst continued to maintain his opposition to the president. As FDR became more concerned with international affairs, Hearst argued that the United States should remain removed from them. This "isolationist" stance partly reflected his own sympathy toward Adolf Hitler's Germany and fear of Soviet communism.

William Randolph Hearst, photographed on vacation in Italy, exercised considerable influence over U.S. affairs via his newspapers.

John, were still toddlers, and I said it was more important that she be with them."

THE RESULT

The result, when it came, was a landslide. Roosevelt won the most decisive victory since 1820, when John Quincy Adams got a single electoral college vote against James Monroe. Roosevelt won in every state except Maine and Vermont. He took 60.8 percent of the popular vote, Landon 36.5 percent, and Union Party candidate William Lemke only 1.9 percent. The electoral college voted 523 to 8 for FDR. In the House the Democrats also triumphed. Their majority in the Senate was so large that 12 Democratic senators had to sit on the Republican side. Landon was later appointed by Roosevelt to serve as the vice chair of the Inter-American Conference in Peru, held in 1938.

ELECTORAL BEHAVIOR

Several important changes in popular voting patterns emerged in the 1936 election. Perhaps the most notable was within the African American community. African Americans had traditionally voted Republican. Republican Abraham Lincoln had abolished slavery; the Democrats, on the other hand, were associated with the racist Jim Crow laws that maintained the segregated society of the South.

The "Black Cabinet" appointments (see box, page 109), along with drives by the NAACP and other organizations to include blacks in politics, meant new votes for Roosevelt. Black Northern

A huge crowd turned out in New York's Times Square on election night to watch results flashed on a giant sign on the Times Building.

the victory was most important because Roosevelt had managed partly to stifle the dominance of the Southern Democrats, shifting the party platform radically toward fully embracing social and racial justice. Roosevelt seemed to be at the height of his popular power.

4. ROOSEVELT'S SECOND TERM

The legislative program for Roosevelt's second term is sometimes known as the third New Deal, though it was neither as dramatic nor as extensive as its predecessors. As his term began, FDR made clear his belief that much remained to be done. In his inaugural speech of 1937 he announced, "I see one-third of a nation ill-housed, ill-clad, ill-nourished…." He outlined a program that would bring a degree of coherent national planning, including a reorganization of the executive that would increase the president's power. However, his

voters were an important bloc in the 1936 election.

Another important voting bloc were American Catholics. Roosevelt had curried favor with them through the old political tactic of patronage. He had appointed 51 Catholics as federal judges during his first term, one in four of his appointments, leading to a sixfold increase in Catholic representation on the bench. Priests praised him from pulpits. Congregations massed in favor of Roosevelt.

FDR's overwhelming victory can be seen as being the result of a wide appeal that transcended class, race, and geography. Perhaps

A Polling Fiasco

The election of 1936 was the occasion of a famous gaffe when the *Literary Digest* predicted that Alf Landon would win by a landslide. The magazine had got the winner right in every election since 1920 and had predicted FDR's winning majority in 1932 to within 1 percent. It was backed up by some regional newspapers. The poll gave Landon himself some hope: "You know, there was really only one time when I thought I just might manage to win that campaign…. That was when the *Literary Digest* fellow sent word that he had completed his straw poll, just before the election, and that I was the clear winner. That night I lay awake in bed thinking who I would name as my secretary of state."

The *Literary Digest* polling was flawed. It drew the names of voters to canvas from telephone directories and automobile owners, meaning that it omitted the opinions of many lower-class Americans. "They had the figures right but the order wrong," Landon later remarked. By contrast the new, more representative sampling method advocated by, among others, George Gallup predicted the right result and would indicate the way forward for opinion polling.

proposed legislation to reorganize the Supreme Court gave conservative Democrats and Republicans an issue on which to unite in their opposition to what they saw as the exploitation of executive power; resistance to FDR's whole program of reforms stiffened.

In fall 1937, too, a new recession drove up unemployment: Two million workers were laid off. In early 1938 four times as many people were claiming relief as in the middle of 1937. Stocks lost a third of their value. Industrial output fell by an average of 40 percent. Now Roosevelt's opponents could argue that the New Deal was not working.

Roosevelt was not sure how to react. On one day, November 10, Marriner Eccles, a treasury official, heard him advocate deficit spending in the afternoon and that evening heard his treasury secretary, T. H. Morgenthau, with Roosevelt's blessing, promise a balanced budget. Eccles recalled, "The contradictions between the afternoon and the evening positions made me wonder whether the New Deal was merely a political slogan or if Roosevelt really knew what the New Deal was."

The combined result of such problems was political frustration and deadlock. The conservatives in the House combined to block the ambitious program of legislation

Roosevelt's Health

To a large extent Roosevelt's disability was ignored by his political friends and enemies alike. The jibe by one enemy that FDR was a "megalomaniac cripple," however, is a reminder of how easy it was for his opponents to suggest that he was not up to the job. In 1935, as opposition to his policies grew stronger, rumors began to circulate that he suffered from Parkinson's disease, a sickness of the nervous system, and from the sexually transmitted disease syphilis. Opponents also suggested that the president had suffered a series of minor strokes. There was no medical basis for any of these rumors.

Just how severely disabled FDR really was remained hidden from most of the American public, but it dominated much of his personal life. After he was struck down by poliomyelitis in 1921, it had taken seven years to return to his political career, four of which he spent at the Warm Springs health resort in Georgia. As governor of New York and president FDR reacted to his illness with courage and dynamism. Newsreporters agreed not to photograph him in his wheelchair or when he was physically helpless, helping deflect attention from the fact that he could only walk by using canes or leaning on helpers. When he did need help with mobility, such as being carried up stairs, he remained unconcerned and continued smiling, putting onlookers at their ease.

Although a cane allowed FDR to give the impression of walking, his progress was slow and difficult. In private he often used a wheelchair.

Memorabilia from a memorable election: The "Roosevelt coalition" forged in 1936 brought black Americans and the urban poor into the Democratic fold.

FDR had announced at the start of 1937, which would have reorganized government regulation of the economy and made it permanent. The Wagner–Steagall National Housing Act of 1937 encouraged the development of some public housing projects, but not in a particularly significant way.

FDR also proposed a new farm bill to replace the AAA and the development of regional bodies to manage natural resources. These were dubbed—after the successful Tennessee Valley Authority—the "Seven Little TVAs." They were never passed. The farm bill, which passed in 1938, was little more than the effective reconstitution of the AAA to take account of the Supreme Court's objections.

DEALING WITH THE COURT

After his reelection Roosevelt proposed legislation giving him the ability to appoint as many as six new judges. If a justice turned 70 but did not retire, he could appoint a new justice. This "court packing" legislation would remain hung up in committee while gradually the older justices retired, allowing FDR to make more liberal appointees to the Supreme Court. Deaths and retirements ultimately enabled him to make seven appointments to the Court during his administration.

THE SOUTHERN DEMOCRATS

Much of the resistance to FDR came increasingly from conservative Southern Democrats. They felt their traditional way of life increasingly threatened. The New Deal had extended federal authority and regulation in an ominous way. FDR's challenge to the U.S. Supreme Court also suggested to them that their status might be under threat; the Court had traditionally helped protect the racial system on which the Southern economy was based. And the election result of 1936 had shown that Roosevelt now had enough popular support without them.

The challenge was enshrined in 1938 in the "Conservative Manifesto" drafted by Senator Josiah Bailey of North Carolina, which advocated states' rights over federal rights, called for lower taxes and a balanced budget, and protested about the creation of a welfare class. The manifesto galvanized opposition to the New Deal.

In 1938, too, Southern senators filibustered an antilynching bill originally introduced in 1934. Bailey explained the reasons: "The proposed lynching bill is the forerunner of a policy studiously cultivated by agitators, not for the purpose of preventing lynching, but for the purpose of introducing the policy of federal interference in local affairs. The lynching bill would promptly be followed by a civil rights bill.... I give you warning that no administration can survive without us."

After the legislative process had ground to a halt for six weeks, the bill was withdrawn. Roosevelt himself acknowledged the power the Southerners had over him and remained neutral in his support of the bill: "If I come out for the anti-lynching bill now, they will block every bill I ask Congress to pass to keep America from collapsing. I just can't take that risk."

THE FAIR LABOR STANDARDS ACT

To some extent FDR got his revenge on his Southern opponents. In 1938 Congress passed the Fair Labor Standards Act, which marked a further step in the abolition of child labor. It affected some industries—but not agriculture or domestic service—and also extended pay and hours regulation to others, establishing a 40-cent minimum hourly wage and a 40-hour maximum working week. The new legislation hit particularly hard in the South, where more than 20 percent of workers earned below the new minimum, and where cotton planters saw cheap labor as the only way they could keep their costs low enough to remain competitive in the marketplace. As he signed the new act into law on June 25, Roosevelt remarked, "That's that." Though it is unlikely that Roosevelt meant it in such a way, the phrase became famous as marking the effective end of the New Deal.

END OF THE NEW DEAL

In 1939 Congress passed a weakened version of the executive reorganization FDR had asked for. Under the influence of the House Un-American Activities Committee of Congressman Martin Dies, which investigated communist influence in New Deal agencies, the House meanwhile cut funding for federal projects. The Federal Theater Project closed in 1939 and others in the following years. The Hatch Act responded to allegations that New Deal money was being used for political campaign-

ing by making it illegal for federal employees—including those working on relief projects—to be involved in political campaigns.

FDR was exhausted by his struggle against the forces of conservatism. He remarked after a grueling tour of the South, where he tried to promote a more liberal form of Democratism, "It takes a long, long time to bring the past up to the present." New Dealer Harold Ickes noted a change in FDR after the long struggle against the Supreme Court. He wrote in his diary, "It looks as if all the courage has oozed out of the President. He has let things drift.... Ever since the Court fight, he has acted to me like a beaten man."

The Second Term

Roosevelt's second term, from 1937 to 1941, marked a running out of steam for the New Deal, first in the face of recession and opposition in the House, and later as Europe's moves toward war distracted the president from domestic reform. Some important pieces of legislation were passed, however:

1937
March 1	Supreme Court Retirement Act
April 26	Bituminous Coal Act
May 1	Neutrality Act of 1937
July 22	Farm Tenant Act
August 26	Judicial Procedure Reform Act
August 26	Revenue Act of 1937
September 1	National Housing Act

1938
February 4	Amended Federal Housing Act
February 16	Agricultural Adjustment Act of 1938
May 17	Naval Expansion Act of 1938
May 28	Revenue Act of 1938
June 24	Food, Drink, and Cosmetic Act
June 25	Fair Labor Standards Act

1939
April 3	Administrative Reorganization Act of 1939
August 2	Hatch Act
November 4	Neutrality Act of 1939

SEE ALSO

◆ Volume 4, Chapter 1, Right vs. Left

◆ Volume 4, Chapter 2, The Supreme Court

◆ Volume 4, Chapter 3, Huey Long

◆ Volume 4, Chapter 4, The Right-Wing Backlash

◆ Volume 5, Chapter 1, Government, Industry, and Economic Policy

◆ Volume 5, Chapter 2, Equality for Some

GLOSSARY

balanced budget an economic term used to describe a situation in which a government's income is enough to pay for all its expenditure. The balanced budget was an essential principle in U.S. economic policy until Roosevelt adopted deficit spending in 1937. *See also* deficit spending.

business cycle an economic term used to describe the periodic but unpredictable and inexplicable rise and fall of economic activity.

capitalism an economic system in which private individuals and companies control the production and distribution of goods and services.

communism a political doctrine advocated by Karl Marx and Friedrich Engels in the 19th century that proposes the overthrow of capitalism and its replacement by working-class rule. Communism was the official ideology of the Soviet Union and was highly feared in the United States.

deficit spending an economic approach in which a government goes into debt in order to fund its activities. Deficit spending is a central tenet of Keynesianism.

depression a deep trough in the business cycle. No other depression matched the intensity of or lasted as long as the Great Depression.

fascism a political ideology based on authoritarian rule and suppression, aggressive nationalism, and militarism.

gold standard an economic tool that used gold as the measure of a nation's currency, so that one unit of currency always bought a fixed amount of gold. It was chiefly useful in stabilizing exchange rates between currencies.

Hundred Days the name given to Roosevelt's first period as president, from March 9 to June 16, 1933, characterized by a whirl of legislative activity. It was named for the Hundred Days of the 19th-century French emperor Napoleon.

individualism a political philosophy that argues that individuals are most effective when they are responsible only for their own well-being and not for that of other members of society.

installment buying a method of buying originally introduced by car companies in the 1920s that allowed purchasers to make a downpayment on a purchase and then pay the balance in a series of regular installments.

isolationism an approach adopted in the United States after World War I that argued that the country should disassociate itself from affairs elsewhere in the world. It led to the U.S. failure to join the League of Nations.

Keynesianism the economic theory advocated by John Maynard Keynes in the 1920s and 1930s. Keynes argued that governments should spend money to maintain full employment and stimulate the economy. His theories dominated most western democracies from the 1930s to around the 1980s.

labor union a formal organization in which workers act collectively in order to protect their interests such as pay and work conditions.

laissez-faire a French term for "let it be," used to describe an economy with no government regulation of business activity. Laissez-faire is an important part of classical or free-market economics, which holds that laws of supply and demand alone should regulate prices, wages, and other economic factors.

liberalism a political theory that emphasizes a belief in progress, the autonomy of individuals, and the protection of political and civil rights; also an economic theory based on competition and the free market.

mixed economy an economy that combines characteristics of a free-market economy—competition, private ownership—with a limited amount of state involvement, such as regulation of business, wage and hour legislation, and a degree of nationalization.

mutualism a U.S. political tradition that advocates cooperative action as a way to lessen the negative social effects of the economy. The mutualist tradition was behind the general acceptance in the 1930s that government had an obligation to look after its citizens.

nativism an anti-immigrant U.S. political tradition that values "real" Americans and their attitudes over those of more recent immigrants. In the late 19th century nativism saw first- or second-generation Irish immigrants objecting to newcomers from southern Europe, for example.

planned economy an economy in which economic activity is controlled by the state. Most businesses are nationalized rather than privately owned, and the government sets production quotas, wages, and prices.

populism a name given to numerous political movements of the 1930s that claimed to represent the common people; populism also describes the beliefs of the Populist Party formed in 1891 to represent rural interests and the breakup of monopolies.

progressivism a political tradition in the United States that advocated social reform by government legislation. Both the Republican and Democratic parties had progressive wings.

public works projects often large-scale projects run by federal, state, or local government in order to generate employment.

recession a severe decline in economic activity that lasts for at least six months

regulation a word used to describe moves by government or other agencies to control business activity, such as by legislation relating to minimum wages or maximum working hours or health and safety procedures.

relief the term most often used in the 1920s and 1930s for welfare.

Social Darwinism a social theory based on the theory of natural selection proposed by Charles Darwin. Social Darwinists believed that some people inevitably became richer or more powerful than others, and that inequality was therefore acceptable.

socialism a political doctrine that removes business from private ownership in favor of state or cooperative ownership in order to create a more equitable society.

welfare financial or other help distributed to people in need; the word is also sometimes used to apply to the agencies that distribute the aid.

FURTHER READING

Allen, Frederick Lewis. *Since Yesterday: The 1930s in America, September 3, 1929–September 3, 1939.* New York: HarperCollins, 1986.

Brogan, Hugh. *The Penguin History of the United States of America.* New York: Penguin Books, 1990.

Evans, Harold. *The American Century.* New York: Knopf, 1999.

Handlin, Oscar, and Lilian Handlin. *Liberty and Equality: 1920–1994.* New York: HarperCollins Publishers, 1994.

Jones, M. A. *The Limits of Liberty: American History 1607–1992.* New York: Oxford University Press, 1995.

Kennedy, David M. *Freedom From Fear: The American People in Depression and War, 1929–1945* (Oxford History of the United States). New York: Oxford University Press, 1999.

Meltzer, Milton. *Brother Can You Spare a Dime?: The Great Depression 1929–1933* New York: Facts on File, Inc., 1991.

Nardo, Don (ed.). *The Great Depression* (Opposing Viewpoints Digest). Greenhaven Press, 1998.

Parrish, Michael E. *Anxious Decades: America in Prosperity and Depression, 1920–1941.* New York: W. W. Norton & Company Inc., 1994.

Phillips, Cabell. *From the Crash to the Blitz: 1929-1939.* Bronx, NY: Fordham University Press, 2000.

Watkins, T. H. *The Great Depression: America in the 1930s.* Boston: Little Brown and Co, 1995.

Worster, Donald. *Dust Bowl: The Southern Plains in the 1930s.* New York: Oxford University Press, 1982

NOVELS AND EYEWITNESS ACCOUNTS

Agee, James, and Walker Evans. *Let Us Now Praise Famous Men.* Boston: Houghton Mifflin Co., 2000

Burg, David F. *The Great Depression: An Eyewitness History.* New York: Facts on File, Inc., 1996

Caldwell, Erskine. *God's Little Acre.* Athens, GA: University of Georgia Press, 1995.

Caldwell, Erskine, and Margaret Bourke-White. *You Have Seen Their Faces.* Athens, GA: University of Georgia Press, 1995.

Dos Passos, John. *U.S.A.* New York: Library of America, 1996.

Farell, James T. *Studs Lonigan: A Trilogy.* Urbana: University of Illinois Press, 1993.

Faulkner, William. *Absalom, Absalom!* Boston: McGraw Hill College Division, 1972.

Hemingway, Ernest. *To Have and Have Not.* New York: Scribner, 1996.

———. *For Whom the Bell Tolls.* New York: Scribner, 1995.

Le Sueur, Meridel. *Salute to Spring.* New York: International Publishers Co., Inc., 1977.

McElvaine, Robert S. *Down and Out in the Great Depression: Letters from the Forgotten Man.* Chapel Hill, NC: University of North Carolina Press, 1983.

Olsen, Tillie. *Yonnondio: From the Thirties.* New York: Delta, 1979.

Smedley, Agnes. *Daughter of Earth: A Novel.* New York: Feminist Press, 1987.

Steinbeck, John. *The Grapes of Wrath.* New York: Penguin USA, 1992.

———. *Of Mice and Men.* New York: Penguin USA, 1993.

Terkel, Studs. *Hard Times: An Oral History of the Great Depression.* New York: The New Press, 2000.

Wright, Richard. *Native Son.* New York: HarperCollins, 1989.

PROLOGUE TO THE DEPRESSION

Allen, Frederick Lewis. *Only Yesterday.* New York: Harper and Brothers, 1931.

Bordo, Michael D., Claudia Goldin, and Eugene N. White (eds.). *The Defining Moment: The Great Depression and the American Economy in the Twentieth Century.* Chicago: University of Chicago Press, 1998.

Cohen, Lizabeth. *Making a New Deal.* New York: Cambridge University Press, 1990.

Galbraith, John Kenneth. *The Great Crash 1929.* Boston: Houghton Mifflin Co., 1997.

Kennedy, David M. *Over Here: The First World War and American Society.* New York: Oxford University Press, 1980.

Knock, T. J. *To End All Wars: Woodrow Wilson and the Quest for a New World Order.* Princeton, NJ: Princeton University Press.

Levian, J. R. *Anatomy of a Crash, 1929.* Burlington, VT: Fraser Publishing Co., 1997.

Sobel, Robert. *The Great Bull Market: Wall Street in the 1920s.* New York: W. W. Norton & Company Inc., 1968.

———. *Panic on Wall Street.* New York: Macmillan, 1968.

Wilson, Joan Hoff. *Herbert Hoover: Forgotten Progressive.* Boston: Little, Brown, 1975.

FDR AND OTHER INDIVIDUALS

Alsop, Joseph. *FDR: 1882–1945.* New York: Gramercy, 1998.

Brinkley, Alan. *Voices of Protest: Huey Long, Father Coughlin, and the Great Depression.* New York: Knopf, 1982.

Cook, Blanche Wiesen. *Eleanor Roosevelt: A Life.* New York: Viking, 1992.

Fried, Albert, *FDR and His Enemies.* New York: St. Martin's Press, 1999.

Graham, Otis L., Jr., and Meghan Wander (eds.) *Franklin D. Roosevelt, His Life and Times: An Encyclopedic View.* Boston: G.K. Hall & Co, 1985.

Hunt, John Gabriel, and Greg Suriano (eds.). *The Essential Franklin Delano Roosevelt: FDR's Greatest Speeches, Fireside Chats, Messages, and Proclamations.* New York: Gramercy, 1998.

Maney, Patrick J. *The Roosevelt Presence: The Life and Legacy of FDR.* Berkeley: University of California Press, 1998.

Roosevelt, Eleanor. *The Autobiography of Eleanor Roosevelt.* New York: Da Capo Press, 2000.

Watkins, T. H. *Righteous Pilgrim: The Life and Times of Harold L. Ickes.* New York: Henry Holt, 1990.

White, Graham. *Harold Ickes of the New Deal: His Private Life and Public Career.* Cambridge, MA: Harvard University Press, 1985.

SOCIAL HISTORY

Clausen, John A. *American Lives: Looking Back at the Children of the Great Depression.* Berkeley, CA: University of California Press, 1995.

Elder, Glen H., Jr. *Children of the Great Depression.* New York: HarperCollins, 1998.

Gregory, James N. *American Exodus: The Dust Bowl Migration and Okie Culture in California.* New York: Oxford University Press, 1991.

Katz, Michael B. *In the Shadow of the Poorhouse: A Social History of Welfare in America.* New York: Basic Books, 1997.

Lowitt, Richard, and Maurine Beasley (eds.). *One Third of a Nation: Lorena Hickok Reports on the Great Depression.* Urbana: University of Illinois Press, 1981.

McGovern, James R. *And a Time for Hope: Americans and the Great Depression.* Westport, CT: Praeger Publishers, 2000.

Patterson, James T. *America's Struggle Against Poverty: 1900–1980.* Cambridge, MA: Harvard University Press, 1981.

Starr, Kevin. *Endangered Dreams: The Great Depression in California* (Americans and the California Dream). New York: Oxford University Press, 1996.

Ware, Susan. *Holding the Line: American Women in the 1930s.* Boston: Twayne, 1982.

Weiss, Nancy. *Farewell to the Party of Lincoln: Black Politics in the Age of FDR.* Princeton: Princeton University Press, 1983.

CULTURE AND THE ARTS

Benet's Reader's Encyclopedia of American Literature. New York: Harpercollins, 1996.

Davidson, Abraham A. *Early American Modernist Painting, 1910–1935.* New York: Da Capo Press, 1994.

Haskell, Barbara. *The American Century: Art & Culture, 1900–1950.* New York: W. W. Norton & Co., 1999.

Hughes, Robert. *American Visions: The Epic History of Art in America.* New York: Knopf, 1999.

McJimsey, George. *Harry Hopkins: Ally of the Poor and Defender of Democracy.* Cambridge, Mass.: Harvard University Press, 1987.

Meltzer, Milton. *Violins and Shovels: The WPA Arts Projects.* New York: Delacorte Press, 1976.

———. *Dorothea Lange: A Photographer's Life.* Syracuse, NY: Syracuse University Press, 2000.

Pells, R. H. *Radical Visions and American Dreams: Culture and Social Thought in the Depression Years.* Urbana: Illinios University Press, 1998.

Pollack, Howard. *Aaron Copland: The Life and Work of an Uncommon Man.* New York: Henry Holt & Co., Inc., 1999.

Thomson, David. *Rosebud: The Story of Orson Welles.* New York: Vintage Books, 1997.

Wilson, Edmond. *The American Earthquake: A Document of the 1920s and 1930s.* Garden City, NY: Doubleday, 1958.

INTERNATIONAL AFFAIRS

Bullock, Alan. *Hitler: A Study in Tyranny.* New York: Harper and Row, 1962.

Dallek, Robert. *Franklin D. Roosevelt and American Foreign Policy.* New York: Oxford University Press, 1979.

Kindleberger, Charles P. *The World in Depression, 1929–1939.* Berkeley: University of California Press, 1986.

Offner, A. A. *The Origins of the Second World War: American Foreign Policy and World Politics.* Melbourne, FL: Krieger Publishing Company, 1986.

Pauley, B. F. *Hitler, Stalin, and Mussolini: Totalitarianism in the Twentieth Century.* Wheeling, IL: Harlan Davidson, 1997.

Ridley, J. *Mussolini.* New York: St. Martin's Press, 1998.

WEB SITES

African American Odyssey: The Depression, The New Deal, and World War II
http://lcweb2.loc.gov/ammem/aaohtml/exhibit/aopart8.html

America from the Great Depression to World War II: Photographs from the FSA and OWI, 1935–1945
http://memory.loc.gov/ammem/fsowhome.html

The American Experience: Surviving the Dust Bowl
http://www.pbs.org/wgbh/amex/dustbowl

Biographical Directory of the United States Congress
http://bioguide.congress.gov

By the People, For the People: Posters from the WPA, 1936–1943
http://memory.loc.gov/ammem/wpaposters/wpahome.html

Federal Theater Project
http://memory.loc.gov/ammem/fedtp/fthome.html

Huey Long
http://www.lib.lsu.edu/special/long.html

The New Deal Network, Franklin and Eleanor Roosevelt Institute
http://newdeal.feri.org

New York Times Archives
http://www.nytimes.com

Presidents of the United States
http://www.ipl.org/ref/POTUS.html

The Scottsboro Boys
http://www.english.upenn.edu/~afilreis/88/scottsboro.html

Voices from the Dust Bowl: The Charles L. Todd and Robert Sonkin Migrant Worker Collection, 1940–1941
http://memory.loc.gov/ammem/afctshtml/tshome.html

WPA American Life Histories
http://lcweb2.loc.gov/ammem/wpaintro/wpahome.html

PICTURE CREDITS

TIMELINE OF THE DEPRESSION

1929
Hoover creates Farm Board
Stock-market crash (October)

1930
California begins voluntary repatriation of Mexicans and Mexican Americans
Smoot-Hawley Tariff Act
Little Caesar, first great gangster movie of the sound era
Ford cuts workforce by 70 percent (June)
Drought strikes Midwest (September)

1931
Credit Anstalt, Austrian bank, collapses (May 1)
All German banks close (July 13)
Britain abandons gold standard (September 21)

1932
Norris-La Guardia Act
Congress approves Reconstruction Finance Corporation (January 22)
FDR makes "forgotten man" radio broadcast (April 7)
Repression of Bonus Expeditionary Force by Douglas MacArthur (June 17)
Farmers' Holiday Association organizes a farmers' strike (August)
FDR wins a landslide victory in presidential election (November 8)

1933
Fiorello La Guardia elected mayor of New York City.
Nazi leader Adolf Hitler becomes chancellor of Germany
Assassination attempt on FDR by Giuseppe Zangara (February 15)
FDR takes oath as 32nd president of the United States (March 4)
National bank holiday (March 6)
Start of the Hundred Days: Emergency Banking Relief Act (March 9)
FDR delivers first "fireside chat" (March 12)
Economy Act (March 20)
Beer-Wine Revenue Act (March 22)
Civilian Conservation Corps Reforestation Relief Act (March 31)
Emergency Farm Mortgage Act (May)
Federal Emergency Relief Act (FERA) and Agricultural Adjustment Admin- istration (AAA) created (May 12)
Tennessee Valley Authority (May 18)
Federal Securities Act (May 27)
London Economic Conference (June)
Home Owners Refinancing Act (June 13)
Banking Act; Farm Credit Act; Emer- gency Railroad Transportation Act; National Industrial Recovery Act;

Glass Steagall Banking Act (June 16)
73rd Congress adjourns (June 16)
FDR creates Civil Works Administration (November)

1934
U.S. joins International Labour Organization
Huey Long launches Share-Our-Wealth Society (January)
Farm Mortgage Refinancing Act (January 31)
Securities Exchange Act (June 6)
National Housing Act (June 28)

1935
Emergency Relief Appropriation Act (April 8)
Soil Conservation Act (April 27)
Resettlement Administration created (May 1)
Rural Electrification Administration created (May 11)
Sureme Court rules NIRA unconstitutional (May 27)
Works Progress Administration formed (May 6)
Federal Music Project introduced (July)
National Labor Relations (Wagner) Act (July 5)
Social Security Act (August 14)
Banking Act (August 23)
Public Utility Holding Company Act (August 28)
Farm Mortgage Moratorium Act (August 29)
Revenue Act of 1935 (August 30)
Wealth Tax Act (August 31)
Huey Long dies after assassination (September 10)

1936
FDR wins 1936 election (November 3)
Gone with the Wind published
Charlie Chaplin's *Modern Times* is last great silent movie
Supreme Court rules AAA unconstitutional (January 6)
Soil Conservation and Domestic Allotment Act (1936) (February 29)
Voodoo Macbeth opens in New York (April 14)

1937
Wagner-Steagall National Housing Act (September 1)
Supreme Court axes NLRB
CIO wins a six-week sit-down strike at General Motors plant in Flint, Michigan.
Supreme Court Retirement Act (March 1)
Bituminous Coal Act (April 26)
Neutrality Act of 1937 (May 1)
Farm Tenant Act (July 22)

Revenue Act of 1937 (August 26)
National Housing Act (September 1)
Start of sit-down strike at General Motors Fisher Body Plant in Flint, Michigan, which lasts 44 days (December)

1938
Amended Federal Housing Act (February 4)
Agricultural Adjustment Act (1938) (February 16)
Naval Expansion Act of 1938 (May 17)
Revenue Act of 1938 (May 28)
Food, Drink, and Cosmetic Act (June 24)
Fair Labor Standards Act (June 25)
Orson Welles' *The War of the Worlds* broadcast (October 30)

1939
John Steinbeck's *The Grapes of Wrath* published
Public Works Administration discontinued
Federal Loan Agency created
Supreme Court declares the sit-down strike illegal (February 27)
Administrative Reorganization Act of 1939 (April 3)
Hatch Act (August 2)
Outbreak of World War II in Europe (September 3)
Neutrality Act of 1939 (November 4)

1940
In California the Relief Appropriation Act is passed, raising the period of eligibility for relief from one to three years
Richard Wright's *Native Son* establishes him as the era's leading black author

1941
American Guide series published for the last time
Publication of James Agee and Walker Evans' *Let Us Now Praise Famous Men*
Japanese bomb Pearl Harbor, Hawaii, bringing U.S. into World War II (December 7)

1943
Government eliminates all WPA agencies

1944
Farm Security Administration closed

1945
FDR dies
Japanese surrender

INDEX

Volume numbers are in **bold**. Page numbers in *italics* refer to pictures or captions. FDR = Franklin D. Roosevelt; WWI = World War I; WWII = World War II

AAA *See* Agricultural Adjustment Administration
ABC1 6:67
Abyssinia (Ethiopia), invasion by Italy 6:31, 43, *53-55*
acronyms 2:43
Adams, James 1:82, 83
advertising 1:*60*, 67, *74*, 75, *79*
African Americans 5:25-31
  in the 1920s 1:56, 61-62
  banks 3:*7*
  in the Civilian Conservation Corps 2:84
  and discrimination 3:14, *15*, *87*, 4:87, 5:*24*, 25-30, 98, 99
  employment 4:*102*, 103, 5:26-31
  and FDR 2:108, 3:87, 6:100-101
  and politics 2:109, 113-14, *116*, 4:*19*
  teachers 5:29-*30*
  unemployment 3:14, 4:87, 103-4, 5:*51*
  unequal wages 5:27-29
  and the vote 5:30
  and welfare 2:109, 4:87, *89*, 5:25, 26, 31
  writers 5:*107-8*
  and WWII 6:*97-99*
  See also Black Cabinet
Agee, James 5:*112*
agribusiness 3:117
agriculture *See* farmers/farming
Agricultural Adjustment Act (1933) 2:88, 3:36-40, 43, *101*
  unconstitutional 2:89, 100, 3:101, 4:31-32, 77
Agricultural Adjustment Act (1938) 3:79, 105-7
Agricultural Adjustment Administration (AAA) 2:33, 88-89, 89, 90, 3:38-39, 60, 100, 4:14, 5:14
  and black Americans 5:29-30
aid
  food 2:*77*, *78*, 3:*13*, *17*, 4:*8*, *80*, *82*
  for Okies 2:75, 3:*74*, *75*, 76-77, 80
  See also charities/charity; New Deal; welfare/relief
Alcatraz 3:*92*
Alger, Horatio 1:9-10
Allen, Hervey 5:108-11
Allen, Oscar K. 4:*50*, *51*
All the King's Men (movie) 4:*61*
Alsberg, Henry G. 5:100
America First Committee 6:61, *80*
American Communist Party 1:40, 4:16, 6:61
American Dream 5:99
American Expeditionary Force 1:33
American Farm Bureau Federation 4:91
American Federation of Labor (AFL) 4:7, *18*, 99-101, 103, *110*
American Guide series 2:97, 5:*100*, 6:113
American Liberty League 2:99, *100*, 104, 3:101, 4:20-21, *73*, 76, 115, 6:104
American Medical Association (AMA) 4:92
American Regionalists 5:75-76

American Relief Administration 1:103
American Scene Painting 5:75-76
American Silver Shirt Legion 3:86
American Socialist Party 1:40
Anacostia, the Bonus Army 1:117, 3:*86*
Anderson, Marian 2:60, *61*, 3:87, 6:111
  and women 6:111
Anschluss 6:34, 36-39
Anthony, Susan B. 1:20
Anti-Comintern Pact (1936) 6:42
anticommunism 1:35, *40*, 41, 4:8
  and FDR 3:86
  and Hoover (Herbert) 3:85, 86
Anti-Injunction (Norris-La Guardia) Act 3:20, 4:16
antilynching bill 2:116, 5:31, 6:*111-12*
anti-Semitism 4:22, 6:37
  in France 6:19
  in Germany 6:*33*, *61*
  and WWII 6:92
  See also Jews
antitrust cases 4:78
antitrust laws 1:12-13, 23, 5:7-8
Araki, Sadao 6:41, 43
architecture 1:68, 5:75
Arkies *See* Okies
Army, U.S. 6:63, 99
Arnold, Thurman 4:*78*
art deco 5:74
Arthurdale 3:*108*, 109
arts 6:113
  censorship 5:72
  independent 5:73-76
  Native American 5:35-*36*
  and popular culture 5:78-79
  WPA programs 2:91-97, 5:61-73
  See also literature; music; photography
Associated Farmers' Association 3:78
Astaire, Fred 5:85, *87*, 88-89, 6:113
Atlantic, first solo crossing 1:69
Atlantic Charter 6:73, *83*
auctions 3:29, *30*
Austria, German union with 6:34, 36-39, *58*
auto-camps 3:63, 64, 72
automobiles *See* cars

Babbitt (book) 1:58, 61
Bailey, Josiah 2:116
Baker, Ray Stannard 1:21
Baldwin, Stanley 6:20
Bankhead, John 3:41
Bankhead-Jones Farm Tenancy Act (1937) 3:111
Bankhead, William 3:111
Banking Act (1933) 5:16, 18
Banking Act (1935) 4:35, 74-75, 5:16, 18
bankruptcy laws 5:10
banks
  for ethnic communities 3:7
  failures 1:87, 88, 2:25-*26*, 3:7-8, 12, 5:*11*
  and FDR 2:25-30, 56-57, 4:14, 63-64, 74-75, 5:17-18, 23, 6:*105*
  and Hoover 5:13-14, 23
  RFC loans 1:113, 4:84, 5:13, 14
  See also Federal Reserve
Barbarossa, Operation 6:75
Barker Gang 3:95-98, *99*
Barkley, Alben 4:41
Barrow, Clyde 3:*96*

baseball 1:*67*-68
Batista, Fulgencio 6:*50*
Beard, Charles A. 6:45, 82-83
beer, legal sale 2:30-*31*
Beer Hall Putsch 6:*10*, 11
Bennett, Harry 3:*85*
Benton, Thomas Hart 5:75
Berkeley, Busby 5:*87*-88, 6:113
Berkman, Alexander 4:17
Berle, Adolf, Jr. 2:11
Bethune, Mary McLeod 2:60, *108*, 4:87, 5:30, *33*, 6:*114*
birth control 5:49
black Americans *See* African Americans
Black Cabinet 2:*108-9*, 4:87, 5:30, 33, 6:112
Black, Hugo 2:41, 4:77
black market, and WWII 6:92, 93
blackshirts 6:20
Black Thursday 1:90-93
Black Tuesday 1:89, 93-96
Blue Eagle, NRA 2:*40*, 87-88, 4:*66*, 5:*14*
blues music 5:78
Bogart, Humphrey 5:93, 96
bombs, atomic 6:86, 87
Bonnie and Clyde 3:*96*
Bonus Army 1:*117*, 3:86, 4:13, *14*, *21*
books 5:54
  See also literature
bootlegging 1:49-50, 3:88
Borah, William E. 1:39, 5:110, 6:45, 61
Bourke-White, Margaret 5:*51*, 72, *102*, 115-16, 6:113
boxing 1:68, 5:*57*
Bradley, Charles C. 2:33
Brain Trust 2:*11*, 12, 5:22
Brandeis, Louis D. 4:24, 32, *35*, 67, 68, 74
Briand, Aristide 4:*11*
Bridges, Harry 4:108-9
Britain, Battle of 6:*64*, 65
Brooks, Louise 1:61
Broussard, Edwin 4:50
Bruce, Edward 2:94, 5:60, 61
Bryan, William Jennings 1:14, 17, 28, 29
  and the Monkey Trial 1:57, 58, 59
Bureau of Investigation (BOI) 3:90, 99
Burke, Selma 5:67-68
Burma Road 6:*70*, 71-72
business
  in the 1920s 1:54-55, 58, 73, *74*, 83-84
  anti-big business feeling 5:21-22
  business-government partnership 4:62-63, 64-65
  failures 5:8
  nationalization 6:109
  principles (1865-1914) 1:9-18
  small businesses 5:44
  under FDR 2:107-10, 4:62-63, 64-65, 73-74, 78-79, 5:21-22, 6:*104*-5
  under Hoover (Herbert) 4:11, 5:13, 14
  See also industries
Butler, Pierce 3:101, 4:*24*, *67*

Cagney, James 5:81, 93, 96
Caldwell, Erskine 5:*102*, 113, 116
California
  migrants to 2:*73*, *74*, 3:57, *62*, 63-81, 5:38-39, 45

call loans 1:82, 92
Calloway, Cab 5:78, *79*
camps, migrant 3:64-66, *71*, *72-73*, *76-77*
capitalism 4:23, 6:104-5, 109
Capone, Al 1:50, 3:*88-89*, 90, 5:93
  soup kitchen 3:*17*, 4:84
Capra, Frank 5:86, 91-92, 6:113
Cardozo, Benjamin N. 1:116, 4:*34*, 67, 68
Carnegie, Andrew 1:10, 11, *12*, 13, 3:11, 4:7, 95
Carranza, Venustiano 1:24, 25
cars 1:*60*, 76, *81*, *82*, 86, *100*, 5:*11*, 58, 6:*34*
  See also motor industry
Carter v. Carter Coal Company (1926) 4:30
Caruso, Enrico 6:*14*
cash and carry law (1939) 6:64
cattle 3:*43*, 53
CCC *See* Civilian Conservation Corps
censorship 5:72, 94
  and WWII 6:91-92
Cermak, Anton "Tony" 2:21, 22, 3:22-23
Chamber of Commerce, U.S. 5:19
Chamberlain, Neville 2:35, 6:39, *40*, 58-59, 63
Chaplin, Charlie 5:89, *91*
charities/charity 2:77, 3:8-9, *10*, 11, 14, *17*, 20, 4:95
  from the rich 2:79
  See also welfare capitalism
Chase, John Paul 3:92-94
Chiang Kai-shek 6:22, 69
Chicago 1:7, 2:77, 3:21-*25*
  Century of Progress International Exposition 5:59
  education 5:44
  immigrants 1:19
children 5:49-50, *53*
  child labor 1:*11*, 21, 73, 2:117, 4:*28*, 83, 5:50
  in cities 3:16
  hobos 3:15
  in musicals 5:*89*
  Okie 3:71
  welfare 4:83, *92*
  See also education
China
  and Japan 6:21-23, *41-42*, *43*, 55, 56, 61, 69, *70*, *71*
Christian Front 6:37
Churchill, Winston 1:78-79, 2:37, 6:66, 73, *83*, *116*
cities
  in the 1920s 1:51, 55-56, *74*, 75
  children 3:15, 16
  and the Depression 2:75-77, *78*, 3:6-25
  life in (1865-1914) 1:16, *17*, 19
  See also poverty, urban
Civilian Conservation Corps (CCC) 2:*41-42*, 63, 81-85, *92*, 3:21, *103*, 105, 4:85-86
  black enrollees 5:29
Civil Works Administration (CWA) 2:*85-87*, 88, 89, 97, 3:20-21, 4:85
  and black Americans 5:29
classical economics *See* laissez-faire/classical economics
class, social 5:42-45
Clayton Antitrust Act (1914) 1:23
Cleveland, Grover 1:11
coal 1:8, 74, 2:*68*, 69
Cohen, Benjamin 4:69, 73, 78

Colbert, Claudette 5:91-92
collective bargaining 2:100, 105-6, 4:16, 70, 93-94, 112-13
Collier, John 5:33-34, *35*, 38
Committee for Industrial Organization (CIO) 4:*18, 101-3, 106, 110*
communism
 and FDR 3:86, 4:16
 in Germany 6:11, *13*
 magazines 5:113, 114
 in Russia 4:*8*, 6:101-2
 in the U.S. 1:40, 4:16, 19
 See also anticommunism
Community Chests 4:82
concentration camps 6:28, 33
Congress
 72nd ("lame duck") 2:19
 73rd 2:31-32, 80-81
Congress of Industrial Organizations 4:102
conservation 3:103, 104
 See also Civilian Conservation Corps; soil
Constitution, and the Supreme Court 4:25-28
construction 1:51, 56
consumer goods 1:*71*
 See also overproduction
Cooke, Morris 3:112
Coolidge, Calvin 1:54, 58, *70*-71, 72, 84, *85, 103,* 6:107
 "Coolidge prosperity" 1:71-73
 and farmers/farming 3:26-27, 34-35
 and Nicaragua 1:72
cooperatives 3:83, 109, 112-13, 114
Cooper, Gary 6:*45*
Copland, Aaron 5:68, 71, 77
Corcoran, Tom 4:69, 73, 78, 5:*22*
corn 3:39, 101
cotton 1:*7, 10,* 74, 115, 2:71, 3:39
 black labor 5:*25,* 26
 in California 3:*68, 69*
 crops destroyed 3:38
 and mechanization 5:26
 pickers 3:63-64, *68, 69*
 plantations 5:*25,* 26
 quotas 3:41
Cotton Club 1:62, *63*
Coughlin, Charles 2:102, 4:22, 57-59, 60, 61, *72*
 radio broadcasts 2:*110,* 6:51
 and the World Court 6:49
country music 5:78
Coxey's Army 1:15
Cox, James M. 1:42, 2:*7*, 8, 52
Cradle Will Rock, The (operatic drama) 5:63-65
Crash of 1929 *See* Great Crash
credit
 post-Crash 3:8
 pre-Crash 1:59, 77, 82, 83, 89
Credit Anstalt (bank) 5:11
Creel, George 1:34
crime(s) 3:*83-84,* 5:92
 business 3:87-88
 espionage 3:99
 and the FBI 3:93
 intellectuals' view of 3:85
 organized 1:50, 3:*88*-99
 political 3:85-*87*
 of poverty 3:*83*-85
crops, overproduction *See* overproduction
crosswords 1:64
Cuba 6:*50*-51
culture
 popular 5:78-79
 preservation of 5:70
Cummings, Homer 2:*27*, 4:35
Cyr, Paul 4:49
Czechoslovakia, and Hitler 6:36, 39, 40

Daladier, Edouard 6:39, 40
dams 2:*37, 38, 39,* 84, *91,* 92-93, 5:*8,* 10, *28*
dance 1:62, *63,* 66, 5:*72,* 77-78
 Federal Dance Project 5:71
Daniels, Josephus 2:52, 53
D'Annunzio, Gabriele 6:*14*-15
Darrow, Clarence 1:59
Darwinism, Social 1:10-11, 4:7
Daughters of the American Revolution 2:60, 3:87, 6:111
Daugherty, Harry 1:43, *44, 53*
Davis-Bacon Act (1931) 4:16
Davis, Bette 5:*86*
Davis, Chester 2:34, 3:43
Davis, John W. 1:71, 2:14, 54, 4:20
Dawes, Charles G. 1:71, 5:13, 6:13
Dawes Plan (1924) 1:45-46, 6:13
Debs, Eugene V. 1:14, 21, 36, 44, 4:16-18, 106
Defense Plan Corporation (DFC) 6:85
deficit spending 5:19, 23, 6:103
DeMille, Cecil B. 5:84, 6:113
democracy, U.S. 6:101-2
Democrats 6:106
 in 1935 2:104-5
 African American vote 2:109, 113-14, *116*
 black 6:112
 National Convention (1936) 2:*106, 107*-10, 6:112
 Southern 2:108, 111, 116-17
Dempsey, Jack 1:*68,* 4:*76*
deportation, of Hispanics 5:39, 40
Depression (1893-97) 1:15-17
Dern, George 2:*27*
design 5:70, 74-75
Deskey, Donald 5:74
Detroit, unemployment 2:25, 75-77, 78
Dewey, Thomas 3:94
Dewson, Molly 6:110
Dietrich, Marlene 5:84-85, *86*
Dillinger, John 3:93, 94-95, *97*
dime, Roosevelt 6:117
discrimination, racial *See* racial discrimination
diseases 5:*50*
 and diet 5:44
 dust 3:53
 in migrant camps 2:*74,* 3:*71,* 73
 of mine workers' children 2:69
 and Native Americans 5:36
Disney, Walt 5:96, 6:113
Division of Investigation (DOI) 3:96
divorce 5:49, 6:94
doctors 2:78, 5:43
Dollar Diplomacy 1:24, 72
domestic allotment plan 3:35-36
Dos Passos, John 5:102-*3,* 112
Douglas, William O. 4:*41*
Drexler, Anton 6:9
drought
 in the 1800s 3:45, 47
 in the 1930s 1:*104,* 110, 2:73, *75,* 3:42-43, 45, 48-49, 102, 105, 5:*48*
 in the 1950s 3:61
Dubinsky, David 4:107, *108,* 110
DuPont, Pierre S. 2:104
Dust Bowl 2:73-74, 3:*44*-61
 migrants from 3:57, *58,* 62, 63-81
Dust Bowl Ballads (album) 5:*117*
dust storms 2:73, 3:*45,* 46, 49-57, 59, 115

Eames, Charles 5:74
Earle, George 6:52
East Coast highbrows 1:47-48
Ebert, Friedrich 6:7, 8
Eccles, Marriner 4:75-76

economics
 orthodox 4:9-10, 23
 and politics 4:9-15
 radical 4:9, 10, 14, 23
 *See also laissez-faire/*classical economics
economy
 after the Crash 1:106-16
 Dust Bowl 3:57-58
 dynamic (1923-29) 1:54, 71-*73,* 78-85, 86, 88-89, 106
 free-market 5:6-7, 8
 government intervention in 5:7-8, 9, 6:*109,* 110
 Gross National Product (GNP) 5:7
 mixed 4:23, 6:109
 pre-Depression danger signs 1:50-52
 weaknesses (1920s) 1:73-78
 and WWI 1:35-36
 and WWII 6:85-88
Edison, Thomas 1:11
education 2:79, 3:16, 71, 4:83
 music in 5:69, *78*
 Native Americans 5:34-35
 and WWII 6:95
 See also teachers
Eighteenth Amendment 1:49
Einstein, Albert 5:52
Eisenhower, Dwight D. 2:81, 6:114-15
Eisenhower, Milton 6:90-91
elderly, the 5:50
electricity
 hydroelectricity 2:9, *38,* 93
 to rural areas 3:*112-13,* 4:*86,* 6:*100*
Eliot, T. S. 1:63, 68
Emergency Banking Relief Act (1933) 2:28, 56, 4:*63*-64
Emergency Committees for Employment 4:12
Emergency Farm Mortgage Act (1933) 2:33, 3:30, 107, 4:89
Emergency Quota Act 1:46
Emergency Relief and Construction Act (1932) 1:114, 4:13, 84
Emergency Unemployment Relief Appeal 4:*84*
employment 5:*48*
 of African Americans 4:*102,* 103, 5:26-31
 middle classes 5:43-44
 of Native Americans 5:35-36
 under the New Deal 2:81-97, 4:*69, 79,* 85-88
 of women *See* women
 and WWII 6:85-86
Espionage Act (1917) 1:35
Esquire (magazine) 5:114
Ethiopia *See* Abyssinia
Europe
 authoritarianism in (1933-39) 6:6-41, *101*
 bank failures (1931) 1:111-12, 5:11
 immigrants from 5:*41*
 inflation (1920s) 6:9, 47
 political extremism (1919-33) 4:8, 6:7-20
 post-WWI 1:44-*46,* 6:7-20
 and the U.S. economy (1920s) 1:78-82, 107-8
 and the U.S. economy (1930s) 5:11
 war loans 1:73, 2:20, 5:11
 See also under various European countries
Evans, Walker 5:73, *112*
evictions 3:9, 22
Export-Import Bank 6:49
exports, drive for (1933) 6:48

Facta, Luigi 6:16, 17
factories-in-the-field 2:*74,* 3:67
Fair Labor Standards Act (1938) 2:117, 4:*28,* 78, 94, 116
families, effects of the Depression on 5:48-50
Family Circle (magazine) 5:114
Farewell to Arms, A (book) 5:104, 6:*45,* 46
Farley, James A. 2:10, 13-14, *27,* 4:76
Farm Board 3:27, 33-34
Farm Credit Administration 3:39, 60, 4:89
farmers/farming 1:56
 and conservation 3:*60,* 61, *100,* 103, 104-5, 104-5, *106*
 and FDR's administration *See* New Deal
 federal aid for 3:60-61, 4:89-91
 golden age 3:27
 and Hoover's administration 1:*102, 104, 106,* 107, 110, 114, 115, 3:27, 33-34
 loans to 3:40, *41,* 114
 mechanization 1:*8,* 3:26, 27, *28*-29, 45, 47, 66, *117,* 5:26
 National Farmers' Alliance 1:14-15
 problems 2:25, 69-75, 3:27-*33, 34, 35,* 102-3
 subsidies 2:34, 88-89, 4:31
 subsistence farming 3:109
 "suitcase farmers" 3:48
 and tariffs 1:104-5, 107
 tenant farmers 2:71-72, 3:*33,* 114, 4:91, 5:25-26
 types of farming 3:28
 See also Dust Bowl; migration; rural America; sharecropping/ sharecroppers; soil
Farmers' Holiday Association 3:29-30, 31, 37
Farm Mortgage Refinancing Act (1934) 3:30
Farm Relief Act (1933) 2:31, 32-34
Farm Relief Bill (1929) 1:*106*
Farm Security Administration (FSA) 3:*41, 61,* 75, *111*-15, 4:90-91, 5:40
Farrell, James T. 5:103, *106,* 112, 113
fascism 6:37
 in Britain 6:20, *37*
 in Germany *See* Nazism
 in Italy 1:46, 6:*14-18*
 in the U.S. 3:86, 4:8, *20,* 22, 6:*37*
Faulkner, William 5:81, *104*-5
FBI (Federal Bureau of Investigation) 3:93, 5:94
Fechner, Robert 2:81
Federal Art Project (FAP) 2:*91,* 94-95, *96,* 5:*60,* 61, 66-68, 70
Federal Bank Deposit Insurance Corporation 6:105
federal camps 3:75-78
Federal Communications Commission 5:16
Federal Council on Negro Affairs *See* Black Cabinet
Federal Dance Project (FDP) 5:71
Federal Deposit Insurance Corporation 4:14, 68, 5:18
Federal Economy Act (1932) 3:13
Federal Emergency Relief Act (1933) 2:36, 3:20
Federal Emergency Relief Administration (FERA) 2:36, 3:23, 39, *40*-41, 60, 4:85, 92
 and black Americans 5:29
Federal Farm Mortgage Corporation 3:30

Federal Housing Administration (FHA) 4:89, 5:29
Federal Loan Agency 5:15
Federal Music Project (FMP) 2:95-97, 5:61, 68-71, 78
Federal One projects 2:91-97, 105, 4:86, 88, 5:61, 62-71
Federal Reserve 1:23, 79, 81, 82, 2:34, 5:16, 6:105
  and the Great Crash 1:88, 89
  and the Second New Deal 4:68-69, 75
Federal Surplus Relief Corporation 3:53
Federal Theater Project (FTP) 2:94, 117, 4:88, 5:61, 62-65
Federal Trade Commission 1:23, 72-73
Federal Writers' Project (FWP) 2:97, 5:61, 69, 100, 107
FERA See Federal Emergency Relief Administration
Fields, W. C. 3:64, 5:88, 89-90
films
  conservation programs 3:104
  documentary 5:72-73
  See also movies
Fitzgerald, F. Scott 1:55, 58, 66, 5:43, 81
Fitzgerald, Zelda 1:55, 61
flagpole sitting 1:63, 64
flappers 1:61, 62
floods 2:93, 3:79, 103
Florida
  Labor Day hurricane 3:103
  land boom 1:76, 77-78
Flynn, Errol 5:85
food 3:10
  aid 2:77, 78, 3:13, 17, 38, 4:8, 80, 82, 5:45
  destruction of 2:89, 3:38
  diet and disease 5:44
  in the Dust Bowl 3:58
  surpluses 3:37, 38, 115
  See also overproduction
Food, Drug, and Cosmetic Act (1938) 4:92
food stamps 3:115
Ford, Henry 1:50, 60, 76, 86, 4:62, 66, 5:18, 21
  and Nazism 4:20, 22
  and U.S. isolationism 6:61
Ford, James 4:19
Ford, Model T 1:60, 76, 86
Ford Motors 1:60, 3:85, 5:17
  immigrant workers 5:52
  unemployment 3:6, 12
  unions 4:109, 114, 115
Fordney-McCumber Tariff (1922) 1:44, 79, 107
foreclosures 3:9, 20, 4:32
  farm 2:33, 3:29-30, 31, 107
Fortune (magazine) 6:52
Four-Minute Men 1:34
Fourteen Points 1:37, 38
Fourteenth Amendment 4:27-28
France 6:47
  post-WWI 6:10, 18-19, 23
  and WWII 6:64-65
Franco, Francisco 6:37, 38, 55
Frankenstein (movie) 5:95
Frankfurter, Felix 4:68
Frazier-Lemke Act 4:32
Freikorps 6:8, 11
Frick, Henry C. 1:13, 4:17, 95
Frost, Robert 5:69
furniture 5:74

Gable, Clark 5:80, 84, 86, 91-92, 93
Galbraith, J. K. 1:86, 95, 5:21
gambling 5:58
games and pastimes 1:63-64
gangsters 3:88-89, 90-99

movies 5:92-94, 96, 6:113
Garbo, Greta 5:81, 84, 86
Garland, Judy 5:89, 96-97
Garner, John N. 2:13, 14-15, 17, 4:41, 52, 5:15, 104-5
Garson, Greer 5:80
Garvey, Marcus 1:51
Gellhorn, Martha 5:107, 112
General Allotment Act (1887) 5:31
General Motors 1:60, 75, 76, 83-84, 89, 2:75, 4:18
  luxury cars 5:43
  strike 4:112, 113
George, Henry 1:12
Georgia Warm Springs Foundation 2:53
German-Americans
  and Nazism 3:86, 99
  and WWI 1:28, 30, 31, 34
Germany
  extremism 6:7-14
  post-WWI reparations 1:45, 111-12, 113, 6:10, 12, 13, 19, 23
Gershwin, George 1:63, 5:77
Gershwin, Ira 5:77
Gifford, Walter S. 1:114
Gillis, Lester 3:92, 93, 95
glass, Depression 5:75
Glass, Carter 4:74-75
Glass-Steagall Act (1933) 1:113, 4:68, 6:105
G-men 3:97, 5:94
GNP (Gross National Product) 5:7
God's Little Acre (book) 5:102
Goebbels, Josef 6:11-12, 32, 33
"Gold Clause" cases 4:33-34
Gold Diggers (movie) 5:87-88
Goldman, Emma 4:16-18
Gold, Mike 5:113, 114
gold policy, FDR's 5:18-19
gold standard
  Britain leaves (1931) 5:11
  Britain returns to (1925) 1:78-79, 80, 81
  Europe leaves (1931) 1:112, 2:35
  U.S. leaves (1933) 2:35, 6:47
golf 1:68
Gompers, Samuel 4:7, 101
Gone with the Wind (book/movie) 5:54, 97, 110, 6:113
Goodman, Benny 5:78
Good Neighbor Policy 1:116, 6:44, 48, 50-51
goons 4:109, 114, 115
Göring, Hermann 6:10, 39
government
  federal branches 4:25
  intervention in the economy 5:7-8
  and the New Deal 6:106-8
  and Social Darwinism 1:10-11, 4:7
  states' vs. federal rights 6:106-7
Graham, Martha 5:71, 72
grain 1:7, 8, 3:101, 102
Grand Coulee Dam 1:116
Grant, Cary 5:85, 90, 92
Grapes of Wrath, The (book) 3:57, 77, 80-81, 5:101
grasshoppers 2:73, 3:50-51
Grazing Act (1934) 3:104, 106
Great Britain
  and the gold standard 1:78-79, 80, 81, 5:11
  post-WWI 6:19-20, 23
  and WWII 6:64, 65-67, 82
  See also London Economic Conference
Great Crash (1929) 1:85, 86-101, 2:25
  affecting Germany 6:13-14

and farmers 3:33
  Hoover (Herbert) and 1:93, 105-16, 3:19, 4:11-12
  predicted 1:82
Great Depression
  end 6:88
  and the Great Crash 1:85, 98
Greater East Asia Co-Prosperity Sphere 6:71
Great Gatsby, The (book) 1:55, 5:43
Great Plains 3:46-47
  See also Dust Bowl
greenbelt towns 3:110, 111, 4:90
Gross National Product (GNP) 5:7
Group Theater 5:65
Grundy, Joe 5:9
Grundy Tariff See Smoot-Hawley Tariff Act
Guam 6:42
Guggenheim, Simon 1:30
guidebooks 2:97, 5:100, 6:113
Guthrie, Woody 5:78, 117

Haiti 1:24, 45, 116
Harding, Warren G. 1:40-44, 53, 58, 70, 2:52
Harlem 1:61-62, 63, 3:7
  riots 5:51
Harrer, Karl 6:9
Harriman, Henry 5:13
Hastie, William H. 2:108
Hatch Act (1939) 2:117, 6:97
Hauptmann, Bruno R. 1:69, 3:90, 93
Haymarket Riot 1:13
Hays Office 5:94
Haywood, W. "Big Bill" D. 1:21, 36, 4:18, 106
health 5:50
  and dust storms 3:53-56
  and Native Americans 5:36
  and the New Deal 4:91-93
  vaccinations 2:74, 3:71
Hearst, William Randolph 2:113, 4:70, 73, 6:49
Hemingway, Ernest 1:34, 68, 5:104, 107, 6:45-46
Hepburn, Katharine 5:85, 92
Herbst, Josephine 5:107, 112
Hess, Rudolf 6:12
Hickok, Lorena 2:73, 76, 3:41
Hightstown 4:90, 5:76
Hindenburg disaster 5:56
Hindenburg, Paul von 6:11, 30
Hine, Lewis W. 1:11, 20, 5:72, 73, 116
Hirohito, emperor of Japan 6:21, 22, 3, 77
Hiroshima 6:86, 87
Hitler, Adolf 1:46, 4:6, 8, 22, 6:8-14, 25-41, 102
  and the Munich Agreement 6:40, 58-59
  and WWII 6:62
hobos 2:67-68, 3:15, 19, 84-85, 5:45
Holding Company Act (1935) 5:16
Hollywood 1:65-66, 5:80-97, 6:113
  See also movies
Holmes, Oliver Wendell 4:24, 28
homeless, the 2:65, 3:14-15, 18, 5:44, 46
  See also hobos
home life 5:45-50
Home Owners Loan Act (1933) 2:37
Home Owners Loan Corporation (HOLC) 2:37, 4:88
Homestead Act (1862) 3:45, 46
homesteads 3:45, 46
  in cooperative communities 3:108, 109

Hoover, Herbert 1:102-5, 3:16-20, 4:13, 15
  and the American Liberty League 4:21
  and the Bonus Army 1:117, 3:86, 4:13
  and businesses 4:11, 5:13, 14
  and communism 3:85, 86
  and Coolidge 1:73, 74, 84, 103
  and economic recovery 1:106-16, 4:10-13, 5:8-14, 23
  and farming See farmers/farming
  and FDR 2:20-21, 22, 26, 5:14, 23
  and government intervention 5:9
  and the Great Crash 1:93, 106, 3:19, 4:11-12
  and Harding 1:43, 44
  and immigration 5:40
  and international debts 5:11
  and Native Americans 5:33
  and New Deal policies 5:12
  and the stock boom 1:78, 88
  presidential election (1932) 2:15, 18
  and unemployment 1:108, 5:9, 10
  welfare under 3:19, 20, 4:12-13, 84, 5:7
  and WWI 1:36
Hoover, J. Edgar 1:41
  and the FBI 3:93
Hoover-Stimson Doctrine 1:116
Hoovervilles 1:108, 110, 111, 3:18, 72, 84, 5:44
Hopkins, Harry 2:10, 11, 36-37, 85, 86, 91, 3:40, 4:85, 5:21
  and Lorena Hickock 2:76
  quoted on censorship 5:72
  and race 5:30
Hopper, Edward 5:76
horror movies 5:94-95, 6:113
House, Edward 1:28, 29
Houseman, John 5:63, 65
House Un-American Activities Committee 2:117, 3:86, 6:102
housing 1:56, 5:46
  and crime 3:82, 83
  evictions 3:9
  in Greenbelt model community 3:110
  homesteads 3:108, 109
  of migrants 2:75, 3:72-73, 75-78
  Native American 5:36, 37
  and the New Deal 2:84, 85, 4:88, 89-91
  and the Public Works Administration 2:84, 85, 4:89
  and relocation 4:90
  rented 2:77
  tenements 1:16, 17, 3:21
  See also Hoovervilles; slums
Housing (Wagner-Steagall) Act (1937) 2:116, 4:89, 91
Howe, Louis M. 2:10, 11, 54
How the Other Half Lives (book) 1:16, 4:82
Huerta, Victoriano 1:24, 25
Hughes, Charles Evans 1:29, 116, 3:101, 4:24, 30, 67
Hull, Cordell 2:27, 35, 6:47, 48, 57, 77
Hungary, fascism 6:37
Hurley, Patrick 1:117
hurricane, Labor Day (1935) 3:103
hydroelectricity 2:9, 38, 93

Iceland 6:75, 83
Ickes, Harold 2:27, 85, 3:23, 4:36, 64, 65, 78, 5:30
immigrants 1:6, 16, 17, 18-19, 46, 5:52, 52
  Asian 5:40
  Filipino 5:40-41

Jewish 5:*41*, 52
  leaving America 5:52
  Mexican 5:37-38, 40
  stereotyping 1:*47*
  and work programs 4:87
  and WWI 1:31-32
  and WWII 6:90, 95-97
  See also immigration; racial
    discrimination
immigration, restriction on 1:46-
  47, 5:37-38, 41
Imperial Way Faction 6:43
imports, tariffs on *See* tariffs
Index of American Design 5:70, 75
Indian Arts and Crafts Board
  5:35-36
Indian Reorganization (Wheeler-
  Howard) Act (1934) 5:33-34, 36
Individualism 3:6, 8, 4:7, 6:108-9
Indochina, Japanese advance into
  6:72-73
industrialization, pre-Depression
  1:6-8
Industrial Workers of the World
  (IWW) 1:*19*, 21, 4:17, 18, 101
industries
  production 4:9
  reform under FDR 5:20
  self-regulation *See* National
    Recovery Administration
  shrinking 2:65, 72
  and WWII 6:*86*-87, 89, 102-3,
    102
  See also business
inflation, in Europe (1920s)
  6:*9*, 47
insurance, health 4:92-93
interest rates 1:81, 5:9, 10
International Labor Defense
  (ILD) 4:19
International Labour Organization
  (ILO) 4:16
International Monetary Fund 6:99
Inukai, Tsuyoshi 6:41
investment trusts 1:84-85
Irish-Americans, and WWI
  1:31-32
iron 1:*7*, 8
isolationism 1:39, 44, *45*, 5:24,
  6:42, 45-57, 57, 60-67
Italian-Americans 3:86
Italy
  fascism 1:46, 6:102
  invasion of Abyssinia 6:31, 43,
    53-55
It Can't Happen Here (play) 5:62-
  63, 65
It Happened One Night (movie)
  5:91-92

James, William 1:12
Japan 1:44
  attack on Pearl Harbor 6:60, 76,
    78-79, *84*, *85*, 116
  militarism 6:20-23, 25, *41*-43,
    55-56, 61, 67-73, 75-79, 102
  sinking of the USS *Panay* 6:*56*,
    57-58
Japanese-Americans, and WWII
  6:*90*-91
jazz 1:62, 5:77-78, *79*
Jazz Singer, The (movie) 1:65,
  5:81, 85
Jews 3:8-9, 5:*41*, 52
  See also anti-Semitism
Johnson Act (1934) 6:48
Johnson, Hiram W. 1:39, 6:*48*
Johnson, Hugh 2:87, 88, 4:*52*, 65-
  66, 67, 5:*16*, 22
Johnson, James Weldon 1:61-62
Johnson, Lyndon B. 2:*109*, 6:115
Johnson-Reed Act (1924) 1:46-47
Jolson, Al 4:*15*, 5:81
Jones, Eugene K. 2:108

Jones, Jesse H. 5:*12*, *15*
judicial activism 4:27-28
judicial review 4:26-27
Judiciary Reorganization Bill
  (1937) 4:77
Jungle, The (book) 1:*20*

Kansas 3:*52*, 60
Karloff, Boris 5:95
Kearny, USS 6:*74*
Keaton, Buster 5:89
Kellogg-Briand Pact (1928) 4:*11*
Kelly, Alvin "Shipwreck" 1:*63*
Kelly, Edward J. 3:23, 24, *25*
Kelly, "Machine Gun" 3:90-93, *94*
Kennedy, John F. 6:*115*
Kennedy, Joseph P. 4:*67*, 69, 6:115
Kerr-Smith Tobacco Control Act
  (1934) 3:41
Keynes, John Maynard 1:45, *80*,
  81, 82, 4:*23*, 5:9, 6:101, 109
  and deficit spending 5:19, 23
King, Alvin O. 4:49
King Kong (movie) 5:85
Kita, Ikki 6:43
Knights of Labor 1:13, 4:99
Knox, Frank 2:111, 112, 6:65
Knudsen, William 6:82
Konoe Fumimaro, Koshaku
  6:71, 77
Kristallnacht 6:*33*
Ku Klux Klan 1:*48*, 58-59, 3:86-87

labor 1:13-14, 4:15-18, 93-94,
  101-3
  legislation 4:115-17
  minorities and women 4:*103*-6
  prominent figures 4:106-11
  and violence 4:*109*, 113-*15*,
    114, *115*
  workers' rights 4:30-31
  and WWII 6:85
  See also collective bargaining;
    strikes; unions
labor camps
  Okie 3:72
  Soviet 6:28
Labor Day hurricane 3:103
La Follette Committee 4:115
La Guardia, Fiorello 1:51-52, 3:*20*
laissez-faire/classical economics
  1:10-11, 12, 72, 4:7, 9-10
  Hoover (Herbert) and 1:107,
    109, 5:8
Lamont, Thomas W. 1:89, 91, 97
land boom, Florida 1:76, 77-78
Landon, Alf 2:111-13, 114, 4:60-
  61, 75-76, 77
Lange, Dorothea 3:*72*, 75, *78*,
  5:*72*, *73*, 115, *116*, 6:113
Langer, William "Wild Bill" 3:29
Lang, Fritz 6:113
Lansing, Robert 1:27
Lateran Pacts 6:18
Latin America *See* Good Neighbor
  Policy
Laurel and Hardy 5:90
Lawrence, Jacob 5:68
League of Nations 1:39, 2:8, 52,
  6:31, 41, 45, 54
  See also World Court
LeHand, Marguerite "Missy"
  2:29
Lehman, Herbert 2:25
leisure time 5:50-59
Lemke, William 2:110, 113,
  4:22, 60
Lend-Lease 6:66-67, 75, 82, 83
Lenin, V. I. 1:46, 4:8
Le Sueur, Meridel 5:103-6, 106-7,
  112, 113
Let Us Now Praise Famous Men
  (book) 5:*73*, *112*
Levant, Oscar 5:77

Lewis, John L. 2:69, 4:18, 102,
  106-*7*
Lewis, Sinclair 1:58, 61, 75, 5:62-
  63, *65*
Liberty Bonds 1:35
liberty ships 6:*89*
libraries 5:54, 6:*103*
Liebknecht, Karl 6:7-8, 11
Life (magazine) 5:72, 73, 113
Lilienthal, David 5:21
Lima Declaration 6:59
Lindbergh, Charles 1:*69*, 3:55,
  5:*77*, 113, 6:61
  baby kidnapped 1:*69*, 3:89-*90*,
    91, *93*
Lippmann, Walter 5:113
literature 1:68, 5:54, 99-111,
  6:113
  See also Federal Writers' Project;
    names of individual books and
    authors
Little Caesar (movie) 5:93
Litvinov, Maxim 6:46
Living Newspaper 5:63
Lloyd George, David 1:30, 6:32
Lloyd, Harold 5:89
loans
  home 2:37, 4:88-89
  RFC 1:113, 114, 4:13, 84, 5:13,
    14
  to farmers 3:40, *41*, 61, 4:90-91
  to Native Americans 5:35
  war loan to Europe 1:73, 2:20,
    5:11
Loans to Industry Act (1934) 5:20
Lochner v. New York (1905) 4:28,
  37
Lodge, Henry Cabot 1:15, 39
Loewy, Raymond 5:74
Lomax, John and Alan 5:69, 70
London Economic Conference
  (1933) 2:35-36, 6:47, 48
Long, Earl K. 4:59
Long, George S. 4:59
Long, Huey 2:*103*-4, 4:22, *42*-61,
  66, 72, 5:*21*-22
  and the World Court 6:49
Long, Rose McConnell 4:49, 59
longshoremen 4:*102*, 109, *113*,
  114
Los Angeles 3:68, 70
  migrants 3:*69*-70, 74
Louisiana, and Huey Long 4:*42*,
  44, 45-48, 50, 58
Louis, Joe 5:57
Luciano, C. "Lucky" 3:*94*
Ludendorff, Erich 6:10
Ludlow, Louis 6:57
Lusitania (ship) 1:28
Luxemburg, Rosa 6:8, 11
lynching 5:*31*
  See also antilynching bill

McAdoo, William Gibbs 1:35, 2:*14*
MacArthur, Douglas 1:117, 2:81,
  4:13, *14*, *21*, 58
MacGuire, Gerald 4:21
McKinley, William 1:17-18
McReynolds, James C. 4:*32*,
  36, 67
Macy's department store 1:*71*
magazines 1:*66*-67, 75, 5:53-55,
  113-15
Mah Jong 1:63-64
Manchuria 6:22-23, 25, 41
Manhattan Project 6:87
manufacturing 1:71, 74, 5:13
Mao Zedong 6:69, 116
Marbury v. Madison (1803) 4:26
March on Rome 6:16, *17*
March of Time (films) 5:82
margin trading 1:84, 85, 88, 92
marriage 5:49
Marshall, George C. 2:81

Marshall, John 4:*25*, 26
Marx Brothers 5:*90*
Marx, Karl 4:*10*
Matteotti, Giacomo 6:*16*, 17
Maurras, Charles 6:19
May Act (1941) 6:95
mechanization 1:50-51, 74
  farm *See* farmers/farming
Meiji, *emperor of Japan* 6:21
Mein Kampf (book) 6:*12*, 35
Mellon, Andrew W. 1:52, 73, 105,
  3:19, 5:9-10, *13*
Mencken, H. L. 1:*57*, 58, *59*, 66,
  75, 103
Mexican-Americans 3:15, 67,
  5:37-40
Mexican workers 3:66, 67, 4:*104*,
  105, 5:37
Mexico
  and the United States 1:24-
    27, 72
  and WWI 1:33
Migrant Mother (photograph)
  3:75, *78*, 5:115
migration/migrants 2:65-66, 69,
  72, 3:32-*33*, 4:*83*, 5:45, *116*
  from the Dust Bowl 2:*73*, 74,
    3:57, *58*, 62, 63-*81*
  novels about 3:57, 77, *80*-81,
    5:*101*
  to cities 2:75-77
  See also Mexican workers
Millay, Edna St. Vincent 5:*105*
Miller, Adolph C. 1:81
Milwaukee 2:90-91
miners/mining 2:*64*, 68, 69, *70*
  See also coal
Mitchell, Charles E. 1:89-90, 91,
  93, 99
Mitchell, Margaret 5:54, *110*, 112
Mohawk Valley Formula 4:113
Moley, Raymond 2:11, 12, 13, 16,
  6:*47*-48
Molly Maguires 1:13
Moncada, José Maria 1:72
Monkey Trial, Scopes 1:57, 58
Mooney, James 6:46
Morgan, Arthur E. 4:87
Morgan, J. P. 1:8, *15*, 17-18, 19,
  30, 4:*71*
Morgan, Thomas 6:46
Morgenthau, Henry 6:*107*
mortgages
  farm 3:29, 30
  mortgage moratorium acts
    4:32-33
  refinanced under FDR 2:37,
    3:30
  See also foreclosures
Mosley, Sir Oswald 6:20, *37*
motor industry
  in the 1920s 1:75-77, 83-84
  in the 1930s 2:25, 75-77, 4:66,
    5:43
  strikes 4:18, 5:*17*
  See also cars; Ford Motors;
    General Motors
movies 1:64-66, 5:73-74, 79,
  6:113
  "B" movies 5:82-83
  California 3:*64*
  censorship 5:94
  color 5:97
  "dish nights" 5:75, 82
  Dust Bowl 3:59
  serials 5:82
  "talkies" 5:81, 82
  theaters 5:*82*-83
  working-class 5:85
  See also Hollywood
muckrakers 1:20, 21
Mukden Incident 6:22, 23, 41
Munich Agreement 6:*40*, 58-59
murals 4:*116*, 5:66-67, 76

Murphy, Frank 4:112
Muscle Shoals scheme 2:38-39, 92
music 5:55-56, 76-78, 79, 117
    European influence 5:79
    See also Federal Music Project
musicals, film 5:87-89, 6:113
Mussolini, Benito 1:46, 4:8, 6:15-18, 31, 38, 39, 40
mutualism 1:6, 3:9, 4:7, 6:108-9

Nagasaki 6:86, 87
National Association for the Advancement of Colored People (NAACP) 5:31, 6:98, 101, 112
National Association of Manufacturers 4:116, 117
National Credit Association 5:14
National Defense Advisory Committee (NDAC) 6:82
National Farmers' Alliance 1:14-15
National Health Survey (1935–36) 4:92
National Housing Act (1934) 4:88-89
National Industrial Recovery Act (NIRA; 1933) 2:41, 87, 106, 4:64-65, 66-67, 93, 101, 115
    critics 2:87, 100, 4:67, 115, 6:104
    FDR quoted on 5:17
    and public housing 4:89
    unconstitutional 2:100, 4:29-30, 115
nationalization 6:109
National Labor Relations (Wagner) Act (NLRA; 1935) 2:88, 105-6, 4:16, 30-31, 70, 91, 93, 101, 116, 5:20
National Labor Relations Board (NLRB) 2:100, 106, 4:30-31, 34, 35, 70, 93-94, 101, 115, 116-17, 5:14
National Labor Union 4:99
National Origins Act (1924) 1:46-47
national parks 5:57
National Recovery Administration (NRA) 2:40-41, 87-88, 100, 4:14, 15, 64-68, 5:14, 16, 20, 21
    and the Supreme Court 2:88, 105, 4:29-30, 31, 34, 67-68, 69-70
National Security League 1:34
National Union for Social Justice 2:102, 4:22, 58, 72, 6:51
National Youth Administration (NYA) 2:60, 4:83, 87, 5:55, 6:111
Native Americans 5:31-37, 38, 71
Native Son (book) 5:108, 109
Naval Act (1938) 6:81
Navy, U.S., and WWII 6:63, 66, 74, 81, 85, 99
Nazism 4:6, 8, 20, 6:9-14, 25, 26-30
    paramilitaries (Sturmabteilung; SA) 6:8, 9, 10-11, 29, 30, 61
    in the U.S. 3:86, 99, 4:22, 6:35, 37
    See also Hitler, Adolf
Nebbia v. New York (1934) 4:28
Negro Theater Project (NTP) 5:63
Nelson, "Baby Face" 3:92, 93, 95
Neutrality Acts/laws (1930s) 6:53, 54, 55-56, 60, 61, 63-64, 82, 84
Neutrality Pact (1941), Russo-Japanese 6:73, 75
Neutrality Zone 6:75
New Deal 1:115-16, 2:13, 16-17, 31-32, 58, 3:21, 4:63-68, 6:102-5
    and African Americans 4:19, 87, 5:26-31

aid for migrants 2:75, 3:74, 75, 76-77, 80
and business See business, under FDR
and Chicago 3:24-25
creating employment 2:81-97, 4:69, 79, 85-88
and crime 3:86
end 2:117, 4:78-79
and farmers/farming 2:31, 32-34, 3:34-43, 60, 100-117, 4:89-91, 6:106
    Federal Project One 2:91-97, 105, 4:86, 88, 5:61, 62-71
health care 4:91-93
and homeowners 2:37, 3:30, 4:88-89
housing aid for farmers 2:33, 3:30, 4:89-91
and housing (public) 2:85, 4:89
industry reform 5:20
and labor 4:15-16, 93-94, 101-3, 116
and Long (Huey) 4:53
monetary policy 2:34-36
and race 6:111-12
and relief 2:36-37, 70, 77-79, 3:20-21, 60-61, 75, 4:84-95
    Second 2:89, 97, 104, 105-11, 4:59, 70-75, 86
and social security 4:94-95
and society 6:109-12
and states' vs. federal rights 6:106-7
and the stock market 4:69
and the Supreme Court See Supreme Court
    Third 2:114-17
and WWII 6:102-3
    See also Roosevelt, Franklin D.; and under various New Deal administrations
New Masses (magazine) 5:113, 114
New Orleans 3:11, 4:90
newspapers 4:58, 5:98, 111-113, 114
newsreels, movie 5:82
Newsweek (magazine) 5:53, 113
New York City
    construction 1:56
    deaths (1932) 2:79
    immigrants 1:6, 16
    poverty 1:6, 16, 17, 3:19, 21
    railroads 1:9
    unemployment 2:75
New York Stock Exchange 1:76, 88, 89, 90, 91, 97-98
    crash See Great Crash
New York Times Industrial Average 1:76, 88, 89, 96, 97, 99
New York World's Fair 5:59
Nicaragua 1:24, 72, 116
Night of Broken Glass 6:33
Night of the Long Knives 6:29-30
NIRA See National Industrial Recovery Act
Nixon, Richard 6:116
NLRB See National Labor Relations Board
NLRB v. Fansteel Metallurgical Corporation (1939) 4:32
Norris (model town) 5:28
Norris, George W. 2:38-39, 5:28
Norris-La Guardia Act (1932) 3:20, 4:16
novels
    escapist 5:108-11
    See also literature
NRA See National Recovery Administration
Nye Committee 6:52-53

Obregón, Alvaro 1:25
O'Brien, Thomas C. 2:110

O'Connor, James 4:51
Office of Price Administration (OPA) 6:88, 93
Office of Production Management (OPM) 6:82, 86
Of Mice and Men (book) 5:101
oil industry 4:65
O'Keeffe, Georgia 1:68
Okies (Dust Bowl migrants) 2:74-75, 3:57, 62, 63-81, 5:50, 101
Oklahoma
    and the Dust Bowl 3:48-49, 51, 52, 53, 57, 59
    migrants from See Okies
Oklahoma City 1:78
Olsen, Tillie 5:103-6, 107, 112, 113
Olympic Games (1936) 6:32
O'Mahoney, Joseph 4:78
One-Third of a Nation (play) 5:63
orphanages 5:50
Our Daily Bread (movie) 5:95
Overman Act (1918) 1:36
Overpass, Battle of the 4:114
overproduction 1:59, 73-74, 82, 86-87, 100, 109
    agricultural 3:32, 34, 38-39, 101
    controlled (agricultural) 2:33-34, 88, 90, 3:41, 105, 106, 107, 115, 4:31
    crops destroyed 2:89, 3:38-39
painting 5:75-76
    See also murals
Palmer, A. Mitchell 1:40, 41
Panama Refining Company v. Ryan (1935) 4:30
Panay, USS 6:56, 57-58
Paris Peace Conference (1919) 6:7
parity prices 3:38
Parker, Bonnie 3:96
Parker, Dorothy 1:62, 66, 84
parks, state and national 5:42, 57-58
pastimes, home 5:52-55
Peabody, Endicott 2:47, 48
Pearl Harbor 6:60, 76, 78-79, 84, 85, 116
Pecora, Ferdinand 4:71
Peek, George S. 38, 41
pensions, old-age 2:104, 105, 4:22, 57, 73, 94, 96, 5:53
Perkins, Frances 2:27, 29, 4:95, 110, 112, 6:110-11
Pershing, John J. 1:24, 25, 33, 37
Pesotta, Rose 4:109-10, 111
Philadelphia, Committee for Unemployment Relief 3:10-11
Philippines 1:18, 6:42, 69
    immigration from 5:40-41
photography 5:71-72, 73, 115-16, 6:113
    See also Bourke-White, Margaret; Hine, Lewis W.; Lange, Dorothea
Pius XI, Pope 6:18
plantations 5:25, 26
Platt Amendment (1901) 6:51
Plattsburg Camps 1:30
pneumonia, dust 3:53, 56
Poland
    and FDR 6:117
    and Hitler/Nazis 6:39-41, 62, 81-82
politics 6:105-9
    competing ideologies 4:6-7
    and the economy 4:9-15, 23
    extremism 4:8, 6:7-20, 101-2
    and labor 4:15-18
    populist pressure 4:22-23
    and race 4:19, 5:30
    right-wing backlash 4:19-22, 62-79, 102-3
popular culture 5:78-79

populists 1:15, 2:110, 4:7, 8, 22-23, 57-59, 72
    See also Coughlin, Charles; Long, Huey; Townsend, Francis
Porter, Katherine Anne 5:105
Portland, Oregon, welfare assistance in 3:11
poster art 2:96
poverty 2:64-65, 4:81
    in the 1920s 1:55
    and crime 3:83-85
    pre-Depression 1:6
    rural 2:32, 3:100-101, 102-3, 107, 116, 5:45
    urban 2:75-77, 78, 5:44
    See also Hoovervilles; slums; welfare/relief
Powderly, Terence 1:13
Preparedness Movement 1:30
press, the 5:98-99, 111-15
    See also magazines; newspapers
price index (1920s) 1:81-82
Principles of Scientific Management, The (book) 4:11, 12
production
    industrial 4:9, 18, 5:7, 13
    See also overproduction
Progressive Era 1:19, 4:7
Prohibition(ists) 1:34, 48-50, 51, 3:88
    end 3:88
Project 891 5:63
property rights 4:20-21
Public Enemy (movie) 5:93
Public Works Administration (PWA) 2:84, 85, 3:21, 4:14, 36, 65, 89
    and race 5:30-31
Public Works of Art Project (PWAP) 2:94, 5:60-61
Puerto Rico 1:18
Pullman Company strike 1:14

rabbits, jack 3:51
race
    and FDR 2:60, 108, 3:87, 5:25, 30, 33, 6:111-12
    and politics 4:19, 5:30
    See also Black Cabinet
racial discrimination
    against immigrants 5:38, 39-41
    in employment 3:14, 15, 87, 4:87, 103-4, 5:25-30
    in farming 3:43
    See also African Americans; Ku Klux Klan
radio 1:64, 65, 5:55-56, 79
    See also Coughlin, Charles; Roosevelt, Franklin D.
railroads 1:7, 9, 5:7
    "Morganization" 1:17
    strikes 4:7
    See also hobos
Railway Labor Act (1930) 4:16
Randolph, A. Philip 4:19, 6:98
Raskob, John J. 1:83-84, 89, 2:100, 104, 4:20
rationing, and WWII 6:93
Rauschenberg, Stephen 6:52
Reader's Digest (magazine) 5:53-55, 114
Reagan, Ronald 4:117, 6:109, 115, 116
recession (1937-38) 2:115, 4:18, 5:22, 23, 6:103
Reciprocal Trade Agreement Act (1934) 6:49, 50
Reconstruction Finance Corporation (RFC) 1:113, 114, 2:34, 4:13, 84, 5:12, 13, 14, 15
    and World War II 6:82
Red Cross 1:110, 113, 114, 115, 2:77, 4:88, 5:7, 47

and drought-relief 2:*75*, 3:*56*, 4:*93*
and gardens 2:*79*
Red Scare 1:35, 40, 41
Reed, James A. 1:39
referendums 3:106-7
reforestation 2:42
Reichstag, fire 6:*27*-28
relief *See* welfare/relief
Relief Appropriation Act (1940) 3:80
religious communities 3:8-9
Dust Bowl 3:58-59
Reorganization Act (1939) 4:88
reportage, and fiction 5:112
Republicans 6:106
and the 1936 election 2:110-11
reservation land 5:31-33
Resettlement Administration (RA) 3:*44*, 59, 75, *107-11*, 4:90, 5:72, 6:*108*
Reuther, Walter 4:107-8, *109*, 114
Rhineland, German reoccupation 6:*31*, 34
Ribbentrop, Joachim von 6:39
Riis, Jacob 1:16, 4:82
riots 3:*85*, 5:51
roads 1:60, *81*
repaired/built 2:80, 88, 89, 90
roaring twenties 1:54-69
Roberts, Owen J. 1:116, 4:*24*, 37, 67
Robinson, Edward G. 3:*10*, 5:*93*
Robinson, Joseph 2:*24*, 4:41, 50, 51
Robinson-Patman Act (1937) 5:16
Rockefeller, John D. 1:10, 12, *13*, *15*, 4:7, 95
Rogers, Ginger 5:*85*, *87*, 88-89, 6:*113*
Röhm, Ernst 6:*29*, 30
Roman Catholics
and fascism 6:*18*
and FDR 2:114
and Nazism 6:29
Rooney, Mickey 5:89
Roosevelt, (Anna) Eleanor 2:*10*, *29*, *44*, 54-55, *57*, *58*, 59-61, 76, 6:*114*
and camps for women 2:29, 4:110
and FDR's inauguration 2:23
marriage 2:*50*, 51
and migrants to California 3:80
quoted on aid 4:*85*
and race 2:60, 3:87, 4:87, 5:*33*, 6:111-12
"socialist" issues 4:14
and subsistence farmers 3:109
and unions 4:*108*, 110
youth 2:49-51
Roosevelt, Elliot (father of Eleanor) 2:49, *50*
Roosevelt, Elliott (son of FDR) 2:*18*, 28
Roosevelt, Franklin D. 1:49, 2:*44-45*, 61-63
advisers *See* Brain Trust
antilynching bill 2:116, 5:31, 6:111-*12*
assassination attempt on 2:*21*, 22, 3:*23*
and banks *See* banks, and FDR
Black Cabinet 2:*108-9*, 4:87, 6:*112*
and communism 3:86, 4:16
critics 2:99-*105*, *101*, 113, 4:95, 6:100-101
death 6:112-14, 115, *116*
and the Dust Bowl 3:*49*
and economics 4:13-14, 5:14-23
election (1932) 2:10-23, *24*-25, 3:20-21, 4:13
election (1936) 2:98-114, 4:60-61, *75*-77, 5:30
election (1940) 5:*22*, 30, 6:63, *65*, 82

and federal regulation 5:14-16
First Hundred Days 2:24-42, 56-57, 3:*27*, 40, 4:14, 63, 68-69, 6:103
foreign policy 6:34, 44-59, 116
Four Freedoms speech 6:117
Good Neighbor policy 1:116, 6:44, 48
as governor 1:93, 112, 2:6, 7, *9-10*, *12*, 54-55
and Hoover (Herbert) 2:20-21, *22*, 26, 5:14, 23
inauguration 2:*22-23*, *24*, 26, 61-62
Indianapolis statement 6:48
and Long (Huey) 4:53-*54*, 56, *57*, *59*
marriage 2:*50*, 51
monetary policy 2:*34*-36
parents 2:45-46
plans to aid farmers 2:*17*, 3:*27*, 31
polio 2:7, 8-9, 52-*54*, *115*
Quarantine speech 6:56-57, 59
quoted on NIRA 5:*17*
and race 2:60, 108, 3:87, 5:*25*, 30, 33, 6:*100*-101, 111-*12*
radio broadcasts 2:12, 28, *56-57*, 98, 101-2, 4:39-40, 95, 5:55, 6:*47*, 107
reputation 6:114-*17*
and the right-wing backlash 4:19-21, 62-79, 102-3
rise to power 2:7-18, 48-49, *51-52*, 54-56
and the role of president 6:*107*, 114
Roosevelt coalition 6:106
Second Hundred Days 4:70-75
second term 2:114-17
State of the Union address (1935) 2:101
and the Supreme Court 2:100, 116, 4:24-25, 28-*41*, 67, 77, 6:*107*
and taxes 1:112, 2:*105*, 4:73, 5:19-20, 43
and welfare 4:95-97
and WWI 2:52
and WWII (build-up to) 6:57-59
and WWII (road to U.S. involvement) 6:*60*, 63-67, 72-79, 80-84, 116
and WWII (U.S. at war) 6:117
youth 2:45-48
See also New Deal
Roosevelt, James 2:45-46
Roosevelt, Sara Delano 2:*45*, 51, 54
Roosevelt, Theodore 1:16, 19-21, 28, 30, 2:46, 49, 6:48
Roper, Daniel 2:*27*, *33*
Route 66 3:*63*, 66
Rumrich spy case 3:99
rural America 2:68-75
in the 1920s 1:56, 59, 74-75
electrification 3:*112-13*, 4:86
health care 4:92
poverty *See* poverty, rural
See also Dust Bowl; farmers/farming
Rural Electrification Administration (REA) 3:*112-13*, 4:86, 6:*100*
rural rehabilitation 3:40-*41*
Ruth, G.H. "Babe" 1:*67*-68

sabotage 3:99
Sacco, Nicola, tial 1:*47*, 5:72
St. Valentine's Day massacre 3:*88*, 89
salesmen, traveling 1:61
San Diego 3:69
Sandino, Augusto 1:72
San Francisco 1:*116*
general strike (1934) 4:109, *113*, *114*

welfare assistance in 3:11
Savage, Augusta 2:*95*
savings 3:7
Scarface (movie) 5:*92*, 93-*94*
Schechter brothers/case 4:29-30, *31*, 67-68, 69-70
Schmelling, Max 5:*57*
Schultz, Dutch 3:*94*
Schussnigg, Kurt von 6:36, 39
Scopes, John Thomas 1:59
Scottsboro boys 4:19, 5:*32*
Securities Act (1933) 4:69, 71, 5:16
Securities Exchange Act (1934) 4:69, 5:16
Securities Exchange Commission (SEC) 3:86, 4:14, 69, 6:105
Sedition Act (1917) 1:36
Seeger, Pete 5:78
segregation 5:*24*, 40
Selective Service Act (1940) 6:66, 79, 84
Seven Little TVAs 2:116
sexual discrimination 3:13
Shahn, Ben 5:*76*
sharecropping/sharecroppers 2:*71*, 3:*28*, *35*, 39, 56, 4:*16*, 91, 5:*25*, *26*
Share-Our-Wealth campaign 2:*103*, 104, 4:44, 52, 53-56, 5:22
shares *See* stock market
Sherman Antitrust Act (1890) 1:12-13, 19
Sherwood, Robert 2:26
Shidehara Kijuro, Danshaku 6:22
Shouse, Jowett 2:*100*, 4:20
Silver Shirts 6:37
Sinclair, Upton 1:*20*, 3:81
Sing for Your Supper (review) 4:*86*, 87
skyscrapers 1:*56*
slaves 2:*97*, 4:26
Sloan, Alfred P. 1:60, 75, 4:*73*
slums 3:*19*, *82*, 4:*64*
clearance 2:*84*, 85, *86*, 4:89
Smedley, Agnes 5:103-6, 106, 112, 113
Smith, Adam 1:*109*, 4:*9*
Smith, Alfred E. "Al" 2:8-9, 10-12, *13*, 14, 54, 4:*76*
and the American Liberty League 2:104, 4:21, 76
presidential campaign (1928) 2:*8*, 111
Smith, Gerald L. K. 2:110, 4:*22*, 55, 60
Smith-Connally Act (1943) 6:88
Smoot-Hawley Tariff Act (1930) 1:101, 104-5, 107, 110, 4:13, 5:*9*, 10-11
Social Darwinism 1:10-11, 4:7
Social Justice (newspaper) 4:*58*, 6:51
Social Realism 5:*76*
social reform (1865-1914) 1:18-21
social security 4:*68*, 73, 94-95, *96*
See also Townsend Plan
Social Security Act (1935) 2:*102*, *104*, 105, 4:22, 35, *68*, 73, 92, 95, *96*, 5:53
and the Supreme Court 6:106-7
soil 3:46
erosion and conservation 2:*72*, 3:*60*, 61, *100*, 102, *104*, *105*, 106, 115, *116*
restoration 3:108-9
Soil Conservation and Domestic Allotment Act (1936) 3:104
Soil Conservation Service (SCS) 3:61-62, 104, *105*, 115
soup kitchens 3:*17*, 4:*84*, 5:*45*
Southern Tenant Farmers' Union 2:*71*, 3:*43*, 102, 5:*26*
Soviet Union 6:101-2
aid to 1:103
and Japan 6:70-71, 73
labor camps 6:28

U.S. recognition of 6:*46*
and WWII 6:72, 73, *75*, 116-17
Spain
civil war (1936-39) 6:*38*, *39*, *54*, 55
fascism 6:37, *38*
Spencer, Herbert 1:*10*
sports 1:*67-68*, 5:*55*, *56-57*
squatter camps 3:*71*, 72
squatters 3:*83*
Stagecoach (movie) 5:*96*, *97*, 6:*113*
Stalin, Joseph 4:*8*, 6:28, 62, 73, 101-2, *116*
Standard Oil 1:9, 12, 21, 82
state governments
aid from 2:77-79, 3:11-12
states' vs. federal rights 6:106-7
steel 1:8, 17-18, 2:*77*, 4:9, *18*
Steinbeck, John 3:*63*, 5:*99-102*, 6:*113*
The Grapes of Wrath 3:57, 77, *80-81*
Stein, Gertrude 5:*105*
Stimson, Henry 1:*72*, 6:*65*
stock market
boom (1924-29) 1:78-85, 86
bull market (1923) 1:*55*
and business crime 3:87-88
crash (1929) *See* Great Crash
regulation by FDR 4:69-70
Stone, Harlan Fiske 4:*24*, 37, 67
stores 5:*44*
streamlined deco/moderne 5:74
strikes 3:*11*, 14, 4:*101*, *104*, 106, 111, *115*
car workers' 4:18, 5:*17*
farm 2:69-71, 3:29, *30*-31
general strike (Britain; 1926) 6:*20*
general strike (Germany; 1925) 6:*11*
general strike (U.S.; 1934) 4:109, *113*, *114*
miners' 2:*70*
post-war (1919) 1:40
pre-war (1865-1914) 1:13-14
railroad 4:7
sit-down 4:31, 32, 111-*13*
steel workers' 4:18
strikebreakers 4:16, 103, 111-12
and women 4:*103*, 105
Strong, Benjamin 1:*79*, 81
Studs Lonigan (book trilogy) 5:103, *106*
Sturges, Preston 5:95-96
submarines, German
WWI 1:*28*, 29
WWII 6:62, *74*, 75
Subsistence Homestead Division 4:90
suburbs 1:51, 56
Sudetenland 6:36, 39, 40, *101*
suffrage, women's 1:20
suicides 3:14
and the Great Crash 1:91, 95-96
Sullivan's Travels (movie) 5:95-96
Sumners, Hatton 4:39
Sumner, William Graham 1:10
supply and demand 1:81, 109
Supreme Court 4:24-25
and the Agricultural Adjustment Act 3:101, 4:77
buildings 4:*26*, *27*, 29
and the Constitution 4:24-28
FDR's attempts at reform 2:116, 117, 4:35-37, 39, 40, 77
and FDR's New Deal 2:100, 3:101, 4:24-25, 28-41, 34, 67-68, 77, 5:30, 6:106-7
four needs 4:33
and Hoover (Herbert) 1:116
justices 4:*24*, 26, *29*
"packing" 2:116, 4:35-36, 38, 40, 77, 6:107
surpluses *See* overproduction
Sussex Pledge 1:29, 32

Sutherland, George 4:*24*, 67
Swanson, Claude 2:*27*
swing (music) 5:78
Swope, Gerard 4:*62*

Taft-Hartley Act (1947) 4:116, 117
Taft, William Howard 1:*20*, 21, 4:*26*, 29
Talmadge, Eugene 2:104, 4:20-21
Tammany Hall 2:48-49
tariffs 1:44, 104-5, 107, 4:13, 5:10-11
　reduced 6:49, 50
taxes
　in the 1920s 1:52, 73
　and FDR 1:112, 2:*105*, 4:73, 5:19-20, 43
　reduced by Hoover 1:109
Tax Revenue Act (1932) 1:112
Taylor, Frederick, and Taylorism 4:11, *12*
teachers 5:43-44
　African American 5:29-*30*
　See also education
Teapot Dome affair 1:53
technologies, new 1:86
Temple, Shirley 5:*89*
Temporary Emergency Relief Administration (TERA) 2:10
Temporary National Economic Committee 5:22-23
tenements 1:16, *17*, 3:*21*
Tennessee Valley 2:72-73, 4:13
Tennessee Valley Authority 2:36, *37*-40, 73, *92*-93, 3:*42*, 104
　and racial discrimination 4:87, 5:26-*27*
tennis 1:68
Texas
　and the Dust Bowl 3:52, 53, *55*, *57*-58
Thälmann, Ernst 6:11
Thatcher, Margaret 6:109
theater 1:66, 5:65, 81
　See also Federal Theater Project
Third International 1:40
Thompson, "Big Bill" 3:22
ticker machines 1:91, *93*, *97*
Time (magazine) 5:53, *113*
time management 4:12
Tin Pan Alley 1:63, 5:78
Tobacco Road (book) 5:102
Today (magazine) 5:53, 113
To Have and Have Not (book) 5:104
Tojo Hideki 6:*77*
Tortilla Flat (book) 5:101
towns
　greenbelt 3:111
　model 5:28
Townsend, Francis E. 2:102-3, *104*, 4:*22*, 57, 60, 72, 94, 5:53
Townsend Plan 4:*22*, 57, *59*, *94*-95, 5:53
toys 5:*53*
Tracy, Spencer 5:81, 95
trade, international
　post-Crash 4:9
　and WWI 1:27-28
trailers, auto 5:*58*
transients 2:66, 3:74
Triangle Shirtwaist fire 1:21, 4:*99*
trickle-down theory 1:73, 114-15, 2:12
Tripartite Pact (1940) 6:*72*, 73
Trouble I've Seen, The (book) 5:107, 112
Trujillo, Rafael 6:51
Truman, Harry S. 6:114
trusts 1:8-9, *14*, 17-18, 19-20, 23-24
　See also antitrust laws
Tugwell, Rexford G. 2:*11*, 13, 3:*108*, 109, 111, 114, 5:11-12, *20*, 6:*108*

and economic planning 5:22
Twenty Second Amendment 6:103
Two-Ocean Navy Bill (1940) 6:65, 71

U-boats *See* submarines, German
Underwood Tariff Act (1913) 1:23, 107
Unemployed Union 4:*85*
unemployment 1:98, 106, 2:*65*, 3:6-7, 8, 13, 14, *16*, *18*, 5:*6*, *10*, *116*
　before FDR's election 2:6-7, 24-25
　demonstrations 3:85
　farmers 3:29, 113
　and Hoover (Herbert) 1:*108*, 5:9, 10
　miners 2:*64*, 70
　and the New Deal 2:*36*-37, 81-97, 4:*69*, *79*, 85-88
　pre-Crash 1:74
　and racial discrimination 3:14, 4:87, 103-4, 5:51
　welfare/relief 2:*36*-37, 70, 3:10-*12*, *17*, 4:*81*, *84*, 85-88, 96
　women 2:*29*, 3:13, *39*
　young people 2:41-42, 60
Union Party 2:110, 4:22-23, 60-61
unions 1:13-14, 4:15, 18, 30-31, 37, 70, 100-102, *106*, 107, 117
　anti-unionism 4:102-3
　women in 4:105-6
　See also labor; strikes
United Automobile Workers of America (UAW) 4:108, *109*, 112, *113*, 114, *115*
United Mine Workers 4:16
United Nations 6:99, 117
United States v. Butler (1936) 4:31
Universal Negro Improvement Association 1:51
urbanization 1:55-56
　See also cities
U.S.A. (book trilogy) 5:102, *103*, 112
U.S. Children's Bureau 4:83, 84
U.S. Housing Authority 4:89, *90*
U.S. Steel Corporation 1:18, 3:10
utility companies, and FDR 4:73-74

Valentino, Rudolph 1:64, 65
Vandenberg, Arthur 2:112
Vanderbilt, Cornelius 1:30
Van Devanter, Willis 4:*24*, *40*-41, 67, *77*
Vann, Robert L. 2:108, 109
Vanzetti, Bartolomeo 1:*47*, 5:72
Veblen, Thorstein 1:12
Versailles, Treaty of (1919) 1:37, 39, 80, 6:7, 19
Victor Emmanuel III, *king of Italy* 6:16, 17
Victory Gardens 6:89, *90*
Villa, Francisco "Pancho" 1:24, 25
voluntarism 4:7
von Sternberg, Josef 5:84-85
"Voodoo" *Macbeth* (play) 5:63, *64*

wages 1:73-74, 4:9
　minimum wage 2:117, 4:31, 37, 78, 94
　unequal for blacks 5:27-29
　and WWII 6:87-88
Wagner Act *See* National Labor Relations Act
Wagner, Robert F. 1:114, 4:70, 89, *91*, 110-11
Wagner-Steagall Act *See* Housing Act (1937)
Wallace, Henry 2:*27*, *33*, 89, 3:35-36, 38, 105, 5:22
Wall Street 1:*87*, *94*, 2:28
　corruption on 4:71
Wall Street Crash *See* Great Crash

War Industries Board 1:36
War Labor Policies Board 4:65
War Manpower Commission (WMC) 6:85, 96
War Production Board (WPB) 6:86
Warren, Robert Penn 4:61
War of the Worlds, The (radio play) 5:56
Washington, March on (1963) 6:98
Washington Treaty (1921) 1:44
Wayne, John 5:*97*
Wealth of Nations, The (book) 4:9
wealth redistribution 4:15, 22
　and FDR 4:73
　and Huey Long 4:43, 52, 53-56
Wealth Tax Act (1935) 4:73
wealthy, the 2:64, 5:*11*, 42-43, 52
　helping the poor 1:11-12, 2:79
weather, extreme 2:73, 3:48-49, 102
　See also drought; floods
Weaver, Robert C. 2:108-9
Weiss, Carl A. 4:59, *60*
welfare capitalism 3:6, 9-11, 19, 20, 4:7, 95, 98-99
welfare/relief 4:81-82, 5:48, 6:110
　for African Americans 2:109, 4:87, 89, 5:25, 26, 31
　for children 4:83, *92*
　for Mexican Americans 5:40
　for Native Americans 5:36
　pre-Depression 4:82-84
　state/local government 2:77-79, 82, 3:11-12
　today 4:82
　under FDR/New Deal 2:*36*-37, 70, 77-79, *102*, 3:20-21, 60-61, 75, 4:84-97, 5:25
　under Hoover (Herbert) 3:19, 20, 4:12-13, 84, 5:*7*
　unemployment 2:*36*-37, 3:10-*12*, *17*, 4:*81*, *84*, 85-88, 96
　for women 4:82-84, 87
　See also aid; charities/charity
welfare state 6:109
Welles, Orson 5:63, 64, 65
Welles, Sumner 6:50, 59
Wells, H.G. 5:56
West Coast Hotel v. Parrish (1937) 4:31
western music 5:78
West, Mae 5:89-90
Wharton, Edith 1:34
wheat 3:*34*, 39, 41
　in the Plains 3:47-48
Wheeler, Burton K. 1:52, 4:40, 6:67
White, Walter 2:60, 6:111
Whither the American Indian? (book) 5:34
Whitney, Richard 1:91-92, 95, 4:67, 69
Wilhelm II, Kaiser 6:7
Willkie, Wendell 4:*74*, 6:*65*, *81*
Wilson, Milburn 3:37
Wilson, Woodrow 1:17, 21, 23-27, 39-40, *42*, 2:52
　Muscle Shoals scheme 2:38
　and WWI 1:22-37, 38-39
wing walking 1:*54*, 63
Wisconsin, farmers 2:69-71
Wizard of Oz, The (movie) 5:96-97, 6:113
Wobblies 1:*19*, 21
women
　in the 1920s 1:60-61, *62*
　black 5:51
　employment 1:52, 61, 3:12-13, 4:104, 5:*47*, 103, 6:*111*
　and home life 5:46
　as investors 1:98
　and labor/unions 4:*104*-6
　and the New Deal 6:110-11
　politicians 6:110-11

suffrage 1:*26*
unemployment 2:*29*, 3:13, *39*
and welfare 4:82-84, 87
writers 5:103-*7*
and WWI 1:*32*
and WWII 6:94-95, *96*
Women's Trade Union League (WTUL) 4:105, *108*
Wood, Grant 5:75-76
Woodin, William 2:*27*, 4:*63*
Woodring, Harry 2:*17*
workers' rights 4:30-31, 67
working conditions 4:99
　and the law 1:19
Works Progress Administration (WPA) 2:*59*, *80*, 86, 89-*91*, 105, 4:*69*, 70, 86, 88
　and African Americans 4:87
　arts programs 2:91-97, 5:61-73
　criticized 4:86-87
　Poster Division 2:96
　and women 6:111
World Bank 6:99
World Court 6:*49*
World War I 1:22-37
　casualties 6:7
　economic cost 6:7
　end 1:37, 38-*39*, 103
　and farming 2:71
　postwar Europe 1:44-*46*, 6:7-20
　return to normalcy 1:38-53
World War II
　and code-breaking 6:76
　in Europe 6:62, 75, *81*-82, 102
　and farming 3:61
　FDR and the build-up to 6:56-59
　Hitler's plans for war 6:35-36
　and the New Deal 6:102-5
　road to U.S. involvement 6:*60*-79, 80-84
　U.S. in 6:84-99, 116-17
WPA *See* Works Progress Administration
Wright, Frank Lloyd 1:68
Wright, Richard 5:*108*

Yalta Conference 6:112, *116*
Yokohama, earthquake 6:*21*
Yonnondio (book) 5:107
You Have Seen Their Faces (book) 5:116
Young, Owen D. 6:13
Young Plan (1929) 1:45-46, 6:13

Zangara, Giuseppe 2:*21*, 22
Zimmermann Telegram 1:33